the healthy Vegan cookbook

the healthy Vegan cookbook

A New System of Whole-Food, Plant-Based Eating

Colin McCullough

2019

Danvers

Vegan Publishers™

Vegan Publishers
Danvers, Massachusetts
www.veganpublishers.com

Cover design by Rachel Adams
Typesetting by Nicola May Design

ISBN: 978-1-940184-55-5

Contents

Introduction

I discovered at a young age that it takes *a lot* of salt and butter to make lima beans edible. I'm sure there is some unpleasant food you were forced to deal with as a child too. And let me tell you, my mom cooked lima beans at an astonishing frequency. Lima beans are supposed to be healthy, but when you have to add butter and salt just to get them down, it really defeats the purpose. I reject lima beans as a concept—a "healthy" food that I almost have to plug my nose to eat, sacrificing good taste for something that's supposed to make me feel good, or at least, make me feel good for not eating greasy fast food. To the idea that you have to give up taste and block your sense of smell to get something healthy down, I reject and condemn you! That idea needs to be chucked in the trash, along with the rest of my lima beans.

So maybe you want to eat healthier, and you're thinking of trying to cut out some meat, dairy, and processed foods. Your cholesterol is too high and your doctor is telling you to eat better, but healthy foods seem like a small death sentence of its own. I'm going to help change that. I can help show you how to make food that is healthy, tastes delicious, and makes you feel great. You won't feel like you're sacrificing, and what's more, you will even *prefer* to eat this way.

Maybe you're a vegetarian or vegan who wants to eat more whole, unprocessed foods and get away from the packaged food with all the salt, oil, and sugar. Do you remember how much better you felt after you stopped eating meat and dairy? When you ditch the processed foods, it is another leap forward in feeling better. But another sacrifice to be healthier? No! I like food that tastes damn good, too damn much. I will show you that ditching processed foods in favor of homemade whole foods is no sacrifice at all.

This Book Is a System

This cookbook is more than a collection of great recipes—it's an overall system to make preparing whole-food, unprocessed meals faster and more convenient!

When I use the word *system*, I mean several things: First, the book's purpose is to provide as many different vehicles as possible for you to add whole-food, plant-based, unprocessed recipes to your diet (for example, bowl meals with sauces, soups, salad fillings for wraps and sandwiches, and veggie burgers are all different vehicles for using the same basic whole-food in-gredients to make meals, while the breakfast smoothies and the healthy snacks share similar combinations of ingredients). Because the book is focused on this system instead of specific ingredients, it's easy to adapt the recipes to meet your individual needs and preferences.

System also means for me the *types* of meals that incorporate whole foods as much as possible, such as smoothies for breakfast, or bowl meals with sauces for dinner. I didn't write a breakfast chapter like most cookbooks with a variety of recipes for pancakes, scones, cereal / granola, et cetera—smoothies are what I have most mornings for breakfast, and I've included thirty-one different recipes for a lot of variety, including many smoothies that taste like dessert (who wouldn't want carrot cake for breakfast?).

The system also includes methods for food preparation; utilizing a high-speed blender to dramatically cut down on prep time, for example, and storage tips, such as freezing sauces in small batches or using ice cube trays, freezing smoothies and soups in Mason jars, et cetera. These tools will make eating unprocessed meals easier and faster.

Throughout the book, I will highlight how each chapter fits into the overall system.

A Note About the Title

Everyone has an opinion about the healthiest way to eat. While this book is called *The Healthy Vegan Cookbook*, I'm not claiming the definitive word on what it means to be a healthy vegan; this is simply one way. For me, the system and the recipes in this cookbook are what make me feel the healthiest; after a few days of traveling and eating restaurant food, I start to miss how good I feel eating whole, unprocessed foods. Current dietary recommendations are to eat five to six servings of fruit and vegetables per day as a *minimum*, but most us of only eat one to two servings per day, if that. So, what if you had a system that made it easier to hit daily target servings? Or what if, instead of the minimum, you ate ten to twelve servings per day? There are many components to being healthy, but what we fuel our bodies with is an incredibly important one. This book is my take on how to feel healthy as a vegan, and my intention is for you to adapt it to what makes you feel healthiest too.

Whole-Food, Plant-Based vs. Vegan

Vegans don't eat or use any animal products, meat, dairy, or any of the ingredients that come from them. It's possible to still eat a lot of junk food if you're vegan. The term "vegan" indicates a lifestyle choice, but as far as food goes, it says more about what you don't eat than what you do.

When you eat a whole-food, plant-based diet, your meals are based on eating fruit, vegetables, whole grains, bean and legumes, and generally little to no oil, sugar, and salt. It's not a food death sentence, I swear—remember, I'm not into sacrifice. It means moving away from processed foods and eating fresh food made at home. But that doesn't mean having to cook for two hours a day or that you have to be a chef. There are ways to make it super convenient and easy, but it takes some planning. Don't worry; we'll cover all that. But the terms whole-food, plant-based only indicate what you eat, not necessarily the ethics behind that diet choice. At this point many people are familiar with the term "vegan," so I still think it's a useful term. I'll use the terms interchangeably. Call me anything but late for dinner!

I'm Not a Nutritionist

It's funny—lots of vegan cooking classes, videos, and cookbooks are done by nutritionists or, at least, self-taught nutrition experts. They will give you lots of nutritional information about the food they're making: all about the vitamins, antioxidants, nutrients, et cetera. But outside of the vegan world, nobody feels the need to have a degree in nutrition to teach people how to make delicious food. I'm not obsessed with nutritional data. I don't believe you need a PhD in order to know how to eat healthy. There are plenty of studies that show that you'll get what your body needs by eating a variety of whole-food, plant-based meals, and if you want to learn more about that there are plenty of other books and online resources to turn to.

My Story

Allow me to take you on the journey of how I ended up eating so far outside the box.

In 1994, I went to a music college that had a large percentage of Asian students, so the cafeteria cooks made most of the food vegetarian. I ate like a king and found that I wasn't missing meat—the food was so good! My classmate Alex was a vegetarian and took a rational approach, asking me, "If you're enjoying the food, eating healthier, and not contributing to the suffering and killing of animals raised for meat, why not be vegetarian?"

Once I was living on my own, I started reading more about vegetarianism. Two books that were significant in my journey were *Diet for a New America* by John Robbins and *Fit for Life* by Marilyn and Harvey Diamond. These books went in-depth about health and nutrition, the mistreatment of farmed animals, and the environmental impact of eating meat and dairy. I was a vegetarian for all of those reasons, but these two books detailed how much the meat and dairy industry are linked too. If you're vegetarian for concerns about health, animals, and the environment, then it's not a morally consistent choice to continue eating dairy. Both books also offered a challenge—just go vegan for thirty days, and see how much better you feel—just try it. I took the challenge, and I never felt better! People ask me if I ever feel tempted to "cheat" and eat something that's not vegan, and I did feel that way sometimes for the first few years, but I remembered the difference of how I felt before I was vegan, and I didn't want to go back to feeling less healthy.

These books also introduced me to information about how our bodies process food and how while we can be omnivorous and process meat and dairy, our bodies run much better without them. In my case, once I went vegan I became allergic to dairy; there were times that I had dairy by accident and my throat started to swell and I had difficulty breathing. That's my body's way of very clearly saying "No way!" (or "No whey," if you like). Nothing like struggling to breathe to take the temptation away, believe me—I'd rather be alive.

When I went vegan, there weren't a lot of vegan convenience foods, so I was on my own. I love food and I didn't have the money to eat out all the time, so I learned how to cook great food at home.

Not too long after that, my two boys were born, and they've grown up vegan. I kept cooking and learning, and I faced the challenge of finding new ways to get them to eat healthy food. When I tried new recipes and the boys asked for seconds (and thirds), I made sure to save them. There were times when the food budget was tight and I would dig through the pantry, pulling together a hodgepodge of ingredients I could find and try to make dinner that everyone would enjoy. Necessity is the mother of invention, right? That experience helped me to be a more creative cook, trying new combinations and relying less on packaged convenience foods.

The next leap forward for me came when I went on the Holistic Holiday At Sea Vegan Cruise, which is based on a whole-food, plant-based diet that also uses little to no oil, salt, or refined sugar. I had heard of it before but thought it seemed like too much of a dramatic change. I went to all the cooking classes and lectures I could on the cruise, and after eating the great meals on board the ship for the week, I returned home ready to get creative and modify the recipes for most of what I made. The changes didn't affect the taste, but I did notice a big difference in how I felt. My skin cleared up and I felt healthier, lighter.

I began approaching libraries and community programs, asking if I could teach healthy cooking classes, and I found that there was a real interest. I started teaching people to make delicious breakfast smoothies that taste like dessert and healthy, delicious sauces to pour over whole-food, plant-based meals that are good enough to make my kids eat kale, quinoa, and beans, and ask for seconds. It was time for me to share what I'd learned along the way to help other people change the way they eat and become healthier, to make healthy food taste delicious, and all in such a way that people didn't feel like they'd be sacrificing anything.

So now, a cookbook. It seemed like every time I taught a class, people would ask if I had written a cookbook. Or at least, what could I recommend? None of the cookbooks I've seen really cover the way that I eat, so I started wondering, if I were to write the ideal cookbook for me, what would it look like? Well, you have it in your hands now. In America especially, we live in a time and place where we many people have access to an amazing bounty of fresh, healthy food. I will help you learn how to use this bounty to create delicious meals; there is a whole world of food to discover!

Food as an Investment

Every year, we put billions of dollars away into IRAs and 401(k)s, planning ahead so that when we retire we'll have assets to draw from. But far too often, much of that money ends up getting used for medicine and medical visits that aren't covered by health insurance. Wouldn't it be much better to use that hard-earned money for adventures with family and friends, and to actually enjoy *retirement*? There are many studies that show the power of plant-based nutrition as medicine, reversing and preventing most of the leading causes of premature deaths in the US. We spend years planning and saving for retirement, but isn't it just as important to invest in our health as much as we do in our wealth?

Food as a Drug

It's interesting that the statistics of relapse for people struggling with drug and alcohol addiction are very similar to those who struggle with dieting and weight loss. It's like you almost need superhuman willpower to stay away from unhealthy food; why else would the relapse rate of diet and weight loss be so high? And the processed food industry knows it. In the book *Salt Sug-*

ar Fat, author Michael Moss talks about how processed food companies like Kraft and Nabisco have small armies of food scientists who engineer their food to be as addictive as possible, to keep us coming back for more. They work on finding the "bliss point" of their product—just the right balance of salt, sugar, and fat that light up the pleasure centers of the brain, the same way drugs do. They know you're not going to eat just three Oreos and stop there; it takes too much willpower.

It's important to take a look at what it takes to permanently break drug addiction and use some of those strategies to break addiction to processed foods, because food really can be an addiction, and simply wanting to eat healthier and relying on willpower alone isn't enough for most people, including me.

When it comes to willpower, it's important to not have problem foods around, so that you don't have to constantly fight the temptation to eat them. I can pass by the Oreos at the supermarket (or just not go down the cookie aisle), but if I find the package at my house I'm going to eat them, and not three per day. Many psychologists would probably say that avoidance doesn't solve the addiction, that it's just a coping mechanism. It works well for me, but I'm buying my groceries and controlling what comes into my house. However, a lot of people don't have that luxury; it must be terribly hard to use that willpower to eat healthy while watching your family and friends eat the way you used to, to open the fridge and cupboards and have the foods you're trying to quit sitting there staring at you. Superhuman willpower is a setup for failure.

I didn't stop eating meat and dairy because it I thought it tastes bad, on the contrary. Before I became vegetarian, I would eat kielbasa by the yard if I could. There was a time when I would walk by the hot dog stands in Boston and be tempted, and I had to find the willpower to keep walking. Just like a drug addiction, I had to get to a point where the part of me that felt like it wasn't worth it got stronger and dominated the impulse to have meat.

That happens over time. You feel so much healthier and stronger that it's just not worth it to eat those foods. It also really helps to be surrounded by family and friends who are supportive of you, even if they don't eat the same way as you.

Breaking an addiction or bad habit is as much about changing the way you think as it is about making a physical change, but the two reinforce each other. It's been a long time, but I can still remember what kielbasa tastes like. But I also remember how different I felt when I was eating it by the yard, and for me it's not worth feeling like that again, nor is it worth a pig's life for me to taste smoked sausage again.

As I said earlier, this cookbook does not present an all-or-nothing way of eating; you may not be ready to go all-in and may want to start with smaller steps, like one plant-based meal a day or a few days every week. I think you'll notice a difference though, an improvement in how you feel, and will naturally keep moving in this direction. I didn't start eating like this overnight, that's for sure, but hopefully some of the things I've learned over the years can help you so that it doesn't take you twenty-one years like me.

A Vegan Sales Pitch

I'm going to make a short case for going vegan; there are plenty of books on all the benefits of veganism for our health, the environment, animal cruelty, et cetera, so I'm not going to get into all that here. I'm just going to give you my personal take.

Given all the benefits of eating vegan, there are only two reasons that make sense to me why people eat meat (everything else just sounds like excuses to me): 1) it's what people are used to eating, and 2) it tastes good.

As I said earlier, I didn't grow up vegan. My idea of ethnic food was pizza and Chinese takeout. How I grew up without eating falafel I can't understand. I thought Indian food looked like various shades of baby poop. I once spent a week of vacation in Nova Scotia when I was nine, eating nothing but cheeseburgers. As a vegetarian years later, I remember the first time I heard the term "vegan" and thought, *What the hell do vegans eat—nuts and seeds all day?* Well . . . yes, sort of . . . but the thought of no cheese? Horror! So yes, I get why it seems like a huge, daunting leap to eat vegan; I stood in that same place once too. It's a funny thing though, when you take some foods off the menu, you'll start trying new foods and making exciting discoveries—the aforementioned falafel, for example. When I'm sitting quietly and looking thoughtful, chances are I'm probably contemplating falafel. Indian food may look suspicious to the untrained eye, but holy moly those spice combinations are heavenly, like no other cuisine. And yes, nuts and seeds can, in fact, rock in a lot of ways, and you don't have to feel like a foraging squirrel or rabbit while eating them.

Meat and dairy taste good—there wouldn't be a multibillion-dollar industry of veggie burgers, hot dogs, and non-dairy ice cream if it didn't. There's even vegan kielbasa (just call it something else guys; it's not even close). Many vegans feel so strongly about the killing of animals that they don't recognize that, for a lot of people, giving up the tastes that they love and grew up with is a really big deal. Yes, there are vegan versions of many meat and dairy products that you can find at the grocery store, as mentioned above, but not many of these come close. I would go a step further and say that it's probably best to skip those vegan substitutes for the most part since they are largely processed, and even though they're plant-based, your body might not know what to do with them.

Given the justification for eating animal products (it's what people are used to eating and it tastes good), and given all the benefits of eating vegan for health, environmental, and animal welfare, the question becomes: is it worth it? If a cow could understand you, would you stand in front of her or him and say, "Sorry, cow, even though I don't have to eat you, I'm still going to choose for you to die because your body tastes good, and that's just what I'm just used to eating. My personal taste is more important than your life and my health." I made the decision a long time ago that it wasn't worth it. So there's my vegan sales pitch. I wouldn't tell you what to do; all I can speak to is my own experience, and given that it's been over twenty years since I went vegan, I'm either really stubborn, or just maybe I've managed to get a few things right.

A Note About Processed Ingredients

I prefer to use whole-food, unprocessed ingredients whenever possible, though you will notice that some recipes in this book occasionally call for using a packaged ingredient, such as extracts or a tablespoon of oil. These additives are always optional; no single ingredients in the recipes are critical, and they can be left out if that's your preference. But I like the extra flavor added from using orange extract in the Orange Chocolate Energy Bites, for example. There are a few recipes, like Seaweed Salad, where a tablespoon of toasted sesame oil gives it the perfect flavor. I'm not a purist! Having removed about 99 percent of oil and processed foods from my diet, I don't feel too worried about using a little extract or oil when a recipes calls for it. So it's your call!

Whether you're new on your journey of health, or have been on your journey for some time, I'm grateful to be part of your experience! Now let's make some great food!

Recommended Kitchen Equipment

Here are recommendations on the tools that will help make the recipes in this book easier to make. Nothing here is essential, though it would be money well spent.

Vitamix (High-Powered Blender)

This is the closest I'm going to come to calling something in my kitchen "essential." I use my Vitamix several times a day for smoothies, soups, and sauces. The downside is that they tend to be expensive when purchased new, often 500 dollars or more. However, you can find great deals online, buy used or refurbished models for much less, or finance a new model over several years.

You can even find Vitamix copies online that are made in China for less than 100 dollars; these aren't the same quality as the original, but at least it's an affordable way to get started. My Vitamix is almost twenty years old and is still running strong with daily use. If you're trying to improve your health, having a high-powered blender is the best investment you can make, in my opinion. Your health is worth investing in! Skip paying for the health seminars and cookbooks, and make this your first priority. Work up to the other kitchen tools if you want, but get this first.

So why is a high-powered blender so important? It saves a lot of time and planning, and if changing the way you eat ends up being a lot of planning and work, the chances of sticking to it go way down! A regular blender can do much of what a high-powered blender can, but you need to soak many ingredients overnight, and you'll burn through several blenders pushing them to do things they're not designed for. Also, the texture of your smoothies and sauces won't be as smooth and creamy. You'll have to mill things like seeds ahead of time, just adding more steps to making meals.

Large-Capacity Food Processor

It's also helpful to have a good food processor that has a large capacity, around fourteen cups. Having to make food in small batches because you have a tiny thirty-dollar food processor is a pain, and you're probably going to burn it out if you use it regularly. Larger-capacity units are usually more powerful and often have better options for adjustable blades. Plus, a strong food processor is key to make fresh nut butters, like raw almond butter, which is expensive to buy at the store and only lasts a few weeks, whereas making your own is quick, fresh, and much less expensive!

Instant Pot (Electric Pressure Cooker)

Instant Pots cook beans and other food quickly, plus you can use it as a slow cooker or with a timer to heat up meals before dinner, automatically. It can even be used to make vegan yogurt. Indian recipes with chickpeas just never came out right for me; at restaurants the beans are softer and creamier. What's the secret? A pressure cooker. One additional benefit of using a pressure cooker is that more nutrients remain in the food than when cooked on the stovetop!

I was initially afraid of using a pressure cooker with visions of my kitchen ceiling covered with exploded food, but with an electric pressure cooker like the Instant Pot, the lid locks in place while cooking, so no explosions.

Air Fryer

This is the newest addition to my kitchen arsenal and has quickly become one of my favorites. An air fryer is basically a counter-top super convection oven that makes "fried" food with little to no oil. I've never used a deep fryer, but what is a true falafel fan supposed to do? The air fryer makes delicious, crispy falafel with very little oil, much better than just baking them in the oven. It makes great fries and crispy bites of tofu, and it works great for many of the Burgers and Balls recipes in this book.

Vegetable Steamer

Whether you use a stovetop steamer or the stand-alone electric variety, a steamer cooks vegetables more gently than boiling them to death. When making bowl meals, just keep adding veggies to the steamer, set the time, and let them cook while working on the rest.

Extra Freezer

Having a dedicated freezer is helpful for the convenience aspect of the recipes in this cookbook. A common complaint of people who try to eat a whole-food, plant-based diet is that meals take too much time. Who has time to spend an hour making dinner every night? Well, not me, that's for sure. But there's no need to sacrifice eating well to beat the clock! I'll go into more detail in the chapters ahead, but most of the meals you'll find in this book are made much easier by utilizing a freezer. The standard refrigerator setup isn't going to be enough space for what you'll likely need, so I would recommend picking up a small chest or upright freezer, which should only use a few dollars-worth of electricity per month if you buy a model made in the last decade.

Hand Chopper

If you need to chop smaller amounts of onion, garlic, et cetera, and don't want to pull out the food processor, reach for a hand chopper. It's also a fast way to chop nuts and turn bars of chocolate into chocolate chips, and you can easily control how fine you want everything chopped.

Immersion Blender

These are great for blending soups in the pot without having to transfer to a blender. This is a necessity for me since I'd otherwise spill half my soup and burn my hand!

Microplane Zester/Grater

This is great to use for fresh garlic and ginger as an alternative to chopping or using a garlic crusher, and it also works for zesting citrus fruits. Some advice though: the zester can't tell the difference between the food and your fingers, so be careful and take your time!

Citrus Juicer

I usually just leave mine on the counter since I'm likely to use it at least once a day. No need for anything fancy or electric—I love my retro, glass citrus juicer. You could use store-bought lemon juice, but nothing beats the taste of freshly squeezed juice!

Apple Corer

This is another kitchen tool that I usually just leave out because I use it so regularly; it makes fast work of coring apples and pears.

Mason Jars and Glass Freezer Containers

I have a cupboard overflowing with pint- and quart-sized Mason jars and lids, perfect for drinks on the go, pantry storage, and freezing soups for later. I like to use the wide-mouth jars, which I find much easier to clean than the regular tapered jars. Glass doesn't take on the taste of whatever you store in the jars, and they're 100 percent recyclable (although those Mason jars are durable as hell!).

Starting the Day Right

Breakfast Smoothies

One thing that guides how I eat is understanding what kinds of foods the human body can use best. For example, raw fruit takes about a half hour to process—piece of cake. My body knows exactly what to do with that, so I start my day with something easy to process, and that gives me plenty of energy for the morning. If your body could talk, imagine what it would say when you start your day with a bacon, egg, and cheese sandwich and a cup of coffee: "What the hell am I supposed to do with *that*?" Your body is an engine, and the quality of food you put in it makes all the difference in how well it runs in both the short-term and long-term.

I'm going to pick on coffee for a minute. A lot of people start their day with a cup of coffee. People love their coffee; I get it. I think of coffee as liquid steroids—it jolts your system and gives you an unnatural boost, but people do it to their bodies over and over again. You can't hit your body every day with one or more shots of adrenaline and not have consequences. I believe that my body is healthiest when I give it the fuel it wants throughout the day, and shots of caffeine (coffee, tea, or soda) push really hard in the opposite direction. I've never been into drinking coffee, but I can appreciate that for many people it would be a hard thing to give up. Still, it's one of the most important changes a person can make to be healthy, and if you eat a whole-food, plant-based diet but still drink caffeine regularly, you may be limiting how healthy your body can be.

When I drink my morning smoothie, I pour it into a quart-sized Mason jar and take it with me, drinking it throughout the morning instead of all at once. This gives me sustained energy through the morning and keeps me feeling full. Let's use the engine analogy again—an engine has an ideal running speed with peak efficiency. Breakfast is a smooth start to getting my body up to a good speed, and maintaining a whole-food, plant-based diet throughout the day keeps my body running at that speed. Just like running an engine into the red zone regularly isn't a good long-term strategy, jacking your body with caffeine into the red zone every morning is a really tough way to push your body into starting the day.

Sure, sometimes I'll wake up on Saturday and make a tasty tofu scramble. When my house is invaded by hungry teenagers, I'll make blueberry muffins. I used to eat cereal, granola, or oatmeal for breakfast, but compared to fruit, those are all too heavy to start the day. So for me, breakfast smoothies are the norm.

Dessert for Breakfast

I could throw some fruit and almond milk in a blender and make a smoothie, but that would get boring fast. I'd rather throw in an apple, banana, carrots, and some spices with fresh almond milk and make a smoothie that tastes like carrot cake for breakfast. That's more my speed. How about a Chocolate Power Smoothie? Key Lime Pie Smoothie? Yep, that's me sacrificing. I've included 31 smoothie recipes in this book so you can have a different smoothie every day for a month, which keeps things interesting and gets you a good balance of nutrition.

Whole-Food Nut Milk

My breakfast smoothie recipes call for blending nuts to make fresh, whole-food nut milk, rather than straining out the pulp or using store-bought nut milk. Leaving in the pulp from the nuts is a key to making smoothies that keep you full all morning, and the pulp has a lot of nutrients and fiber.

Sweeteners

My go-to for sweetener for smoothies is dates, usually the larger Medjool dates. The dates add a lot of sweetness and are a whole food, so they won't affect your blood sugar in the same way as processed sweeteners like agave, maple syrup, or brown rice syrup. If you're using a standard blender, soaking the dates in warm water for 15 minutes will soften them and make them easier to blend. Don't forget to take out the pits, because even the most powerful blender will just break it down into hard little bits!

Get Creative!

For many of my smoothie recipes, I tried to work out the essential tastes and ingredients that turn a dessert into a smoothie. Let's break down the Carrot Cake Smoothie, for an example: Almond milk makes a good base, carrots are for flavor and color, the banana adds creaminess, and the apple adds sweetness and fiber. The dates add more sweetness, vanilla gives it a cake flavor, the spices make it taste specifically like carrot cake (which usually includes cinnamon, ginger, nutmeg, and cloves), and the flax seeds add more nutrition. You can take any dessert and try to break down the different tastes and textures, and then color-combine ingredients to re-create that dessert as a smoothie!

I use a lot of different nuts in the smoothie recipes; the idea is to provide some healthy fats and make a creamier texture. Some people, though, experience indigestion with some kinds of nuts. This can be minimized by soaking the nuts overnight, which reduces the phytic acid that makes them harder to digest. For those who are truly allergic to nuts, here are a few whole-food alternatives that I would suggest using as an alternative to nuts in a recipe:

- *Coconut Butter / Coconut Manna* is essentially ground/pureed coconut meat, made in the same way as nut butters with a food processor: blending and stirring until the coconut creams to a butter consistency and the oils are released. You can use fresh coconut or shredded, dried coconut in a food processor to make coconut butter, and this will store in the refrigerator for several weeks. Alternatively, you can buy jars of coconut butter in stores or online. Coconut butter is a whole-food, unrefined product, unlike coconut oil.

- *Avocado* can also be used instead of nuts, but it may change the taste and color of your smoothie. Also, keeping avocado on hand for small amounts can be inconvenient, since the window to use a ripe avocado is painfully short. Avocados can be mashed and added to ice cube trays and then frozen and kept in a freezer bag to use in small amounts as needed, which makes it more convenient to use and produces less waste.

Smoothie Tips and Strategies

Adding fruits and veggies: Some fruit and vegetables have a mild taste in smaller amounts and can be included in your smoothie as filler, which provides more chances to include fruit and veggies into your day! Examples are bananas, apples, pears, mangos, and spinach. Frozen bananas and mangos are also great for adding creaminess to smoothies.

Prepping bananas: Buy a bunch of bananas, and when they ripen to be yellow with small brown spots, peel them and break in half, then store in the freezer in a large resealable bag.

Adding seeds: Mixing seeds into your smoothies is a great way to sneak in some extra nutrition without affecting the taste. Examples are flax, hemp, and chia seeds. Hard seeds like flax will need to be ground (use a small electric coffee or spice grinder) first unless you have a high-powered blender. I often see recipes for smoothies that call for protein powders, which aren't something I find necessary. Usually my smoothies use nuts as a base and often call for a tablespoon of seeds like flax, all of which are whole-food, unprocessed forms of protein. Beyond breakfast, I usually eat a variety of whole foods that give me plenty of protein; I don't see any reason to worry and add a processed protein powder to my smoothies. I've seen different recipes for homemade protein powders, but it's usually what I'm already adding to my smoothies anyway.

Adding natural flavorings: You'll notice that in some of my smoothie recipes I use different extracts and natural flavorings—how does that fit into a whole-food way of eating? Well, I'll say again that I'm not a purist. If I can add a few drops of natural flavoring to get the taste I want, I'm not going to worry about it. Sometimes adding a little bit of extract can give the smoothie a real punch of flavor, like natural raspberry flavoring, for example.

Freezing smoothies: an alternative to making smoothies every morning is to batch-process ingredients to make enough smoothies for several days in a row, and store them in Mason jars in the freezer. Take the Mason jar out of the freezer before going to sleep and let it defrost overnight, then it will be ready for you when you head out the door in the morning; just remember to shake it well before drinking. Make sure not to fill the Mason jar past the freeze-fill line, which is right below the point where the threads for the lid begin (this allows enough room for the liquid to expand when it freezes). Or, you can divide the smoothie into pint-sized Mason jars and store them in the freezer, and as you keep adding different smoothies to the freezer, you can mix it up each morning—grab two different smoothie pints the night before to defrost!

Soaking your nuts: If you don't have a high-speed blender like a Vitamix, soaking nuts for several hours will soften them to make blending easier. Also, for people who get indigestion from eating nuts, oftentimes soaking the nuts for several hours will remove a lot of the phytic acid that makes them harder for some people to digest.

Criticism of Drinking Smoothies

Many nutritionists and health food advocates are not especially on board with the idea of drinking smoothies regularly. Critics say that consuming fruit in liquid form is an easy way to consume too much fruit too quickly. My smoothies don't have more than what I would normally consume for fruit in one meal, and I suggest drinking it slowly over several hours instead of gulping it down all at once.

They also argue that consuming fruit spikes your blood sugar. Two points here: First, drinking a smoothie over a few hours helps maintain blood sugar levels so you don't have spikes, and it also keeps you full through the morning. Second, some diets consider fruit to be the same as any other sugar and recommend avoiding them, but that is not what the science shows. Granulated sugar and corn syrup spike your blood sugar levels for a little while, then your blood sugar drops down below what it was before you had the sugar, putting your body into a diabetic state that triggers the production of insulation to get your blood sugar back to normal. This is what you experience as the sugar high followed by the sugar crash. Many studies show that eating fruit, especially if you eat it quickly, will spike your blood sugar, though not as much as processed sugar, but after the spike your blood sugar returns to previous normal sugar levels and you don't experience a crash. When you consume a smoothie over a few hours, it minimizes the spike in the blood sugar and gives you easy energy throughout the morning.

Many smoothie recipes have unhealthy base ingredients, like fruit juice, dairy (milk and yogurt), and added sweeteners, but you won't find that in any of the recipes here.

Breakfast Smoothies as a System

Each of these smoothie recipes makes about 1 quart. I often pour them into two pint-sized jars, taking one with me in the morning and freezing the other or leaving it in the fridge for the next day. I love having a freezer shelf full of smoothies to choose from. Mix and match for variety!

Have you read somewhere that you should include flax seeds in your diet every day? These smoothie recipes are a great way to add in healthy ingredients in small amounts without affecting the taste!

Breakfast Smoothies

Carrot Cake Smoothie

This smoothie is a long-time favorite of the boys. Dessert for breakfast? You bet! I love watching people's faces when they try this smoothie at my cooking classes; how can something this delicious be healthy?

MAKES 2 PINTS

⅓ cup raw almonds
2 cups water
1 apple, cored and sliced
1 medium carrot, unpeeled
1 frozen banana
2 Medjool dates
1 Tbsp flax seeds
1 tsp vanilla extract
½ tsp ground cinnamon
½" fresh ginger or ¼" tsp powdered ginger
⅛ tsp ground nutmeg
⅛ tsp ground cloves

Add the almonds and water and blend for 1 minute, then add the remaining ingredients. Blend for several minutes until smooth.

Note: If you don't have a powerful blender, soak the dates for several hours first, and put the flax seeds in a coffee grinder to grind to powder (ground flax seeds can keep in the refrigerator for several weeks).

Blueberry Lavender Smoothie

This smoothie has a lot going on—it's sweet but also lemony tart, and its bold blueberry flavor is backed up with a hint of lavender. It's complicated but delicious.

MAKES 2 PINTS

⅓ cup raw walnuts
2 cups water
½ frozen banana
1½ cups frozen blueberries
3 Medjool dates
1 Tbsp flax seeds
1 tsp vanilla extract
½ tsp dried lavender flower buds
Zest of ½ lemon

Blend the walnuts with the water for 2 minutes, then add the remaining ingredients and blend for an additional 2 minutes until smooth.

Note: Use dried, organic lavender flowers that are specifically for culinary use; they can be purchased online. Just ½ teaspoon is enough to give the smoothie a perfect lavender accent without making it taste like perfume!

Chocolate Power Smoothie

This smoothie is a nutritional powerhouse, but it's chocolate for break-fast.

MAKES 2 PINTS

⅓ cup raw almonds
2 cups water
1 frozen banana
1 cup packed fresh or frozen spinach
2 cups frozen blueberries
4 Medjool dates
3 heaping Tbsp raw cacao powder
1 Tbsp flax seeds

Blend the almonds and water together for 1 minute. Add the remaining ingredients and blend for several minutes until completely smooth.

Indian Spice Smoothie

*I love the complex flavors of Indian masala spice tea, but can I get
that in a healthy breakfast smoothie? Done!*

MAKES 2 PINTS

⅓ cup raw cashews
2 cups water (steeped with 2 chai tea bags for 5 minutes, optional)
1½ cup frozen mango chunks
½ frozen banana
1" fresh ginger
Juice of ½ lemon
3 Medjool dates
1 Tbsp flax seeds
1 tsp ground cardamom
½ tsp ground cinnamon
½ tsp turmeric powder
⅛ tsp ground cloves
⅛ tsp ground nutmeg
⅛ tsp ground allspice

Blend the cashews and water for 2 minutes, then add remaining
ingredients and blend for 2 more minutes

Note: Replace 1 cup of water with 1 cup Vegan Yogurt (see **Odds
and Ends**) for extra tang!

Key Lime Pie Smoothie

In one of my cooking classes, someone asked if I could make a smoothie that tastes like key lime pie, her favorite. Happy to oblige, Dawn!

MAKES 2 PINTS

⅓ cup raw cashews
2 cups water
½ frozen banana
1 cup packed fresh or frozen spinach
½ ripe avocado
3 Medjool dates
Zest of ½ lime
Juice of 1 lime
1 Tbsp hemp seeds
1 tsp vanilla extract
Pinch of sea salt
1–2 squares graham cracker, crushed

Blend all ingredients except the graham cracker. Pour into glass and crumble 1 or 2 squares of graham cracker on top.

Note: Okay, so graham crackers are not a whole food—you got me. But it *makes* this smoothie. As I said, I'm not a purist!

Oatmeal Cookie Smoothie

Here's a way to have cookies for breakfast but in a way that would get the approval of my mom!

MAKES 2 PINTS

¼ cup raw walnuts
¼ cup rolled oats
2 cups water
1 frozen banana
¼ cup raisins
1 Tbsp hemp seeds
1 Tbsp blackstrap molasses
1 tsp vanilla extract
½ tsp ground cinnamon
Pinch of sea salt

Blend the walnuts and oats with the water for 2 minutes, then add the remaining ingredients and blend for an additional minute.

Note: Hemp seeds (or hemp hearts) have a mild flavor but are a nutritional powerhouse; I regularly add a tablespoon to smoothies for a shot of extra nutrition and protein.

Orange Creamsicle Smoothie

This is a class favorite—an orange creamsicle in a glass! This smoothie is a great way to get some fresh oranges on the go for breakfast!

MAKES 2 PINTS

⅓ cup raw almonds
2 cups water
1 large orange, or 3 mandarins or clementines, peeled with seeds removed
1 frozen banana
½ medium unpeeled carrot
3 Medjool dates
1 Tbsp hemp seeds
1 tsp vanilla extract
⅛ tsp turmeric powder
A few drops orange extract or ¼ tsp orange zest (or both!)

Blend the almonds and water together for 1 minute, then add the remaining ingredients and blend until smooth.

Note: Replace 1 cup of the almond milk with Vegan Yogurt (see **Odds and Ends**) for extra tang.

Persian Smoothie

Rose is a popular flavor in Turkey and Iran, along with pistachios, strawberries, and sweet dates. This smoothie is a trip to another place!

MAKES 2 PINTS

⅓ cup raw pistachios
2 cups water
1 cup strawberries, fresh or frozen
1 frozen banana
3 Medjool dates
1 Tbsp hemp seeds
2 tsp vanilla extract
2 tsp rose water
½ tsp ground cardamom
½ tsp almond extract

Blend the pistachios and water in a high-speed blender for 2 minutes, then add the remaining ingredients and blend for an additional 2 minutes.

Note: You can find rose water at supermarkets in the international section, at Indian supermarkets, or online.

Italian Cookie Dough Smoothie

Let's take cookie dough flavor to the next level with Italian *cookie dough—the taste of buttery almond biscotti and the sweet licorice taste of pizzelles!*

MAKES 2 PINTS

⅓ cup raw almonds
2 cups water
4 Medjool dates
1 frozen banana
1 cup frozen mango chunks
1 Tbsp flax seeds
1 tsp Nutiva Coconut Buttery Spread
1 tsp vanilla extract
¼ tsp turmeric powder
¼ tsp almond extract
⅛ tsp anise extract

Blend the almonds and water for 1 minute, then add the remaining ingredients and blend for an additional 2 minutes.

Piña Colada Smoothie

Start your day on island time, where the pace is slower and life tastes like coconuts.

MAKES 2 PINTS

Coconut meat of ⅛ fresh coconut, or ⅓ cup shredded dried
        coconut, unsweetened
2 cups coconut water
1 cup frozen pineapple
½ cup frozen mango chunks
3 Medjool dates
Juice of ½ lime
1 Tbsp hemp seeds

Blend the coconut and water for 2 minutes; you can strain the coconut pulp from the blended liquid at this point with a fine mesh strainer, or leave it in (it's more nutritious and helps with satiety to leave the pulp in). Add the remaining ingredients and blend for an additional 2 minutes.

Note: Fresh coconut meat keeps well in the freezer, so I like to buy fresh coconut and break it into small chunks and store them in a resealable bag in the freezer to use as needed.

Super-Pink Strawberry Smoothie

This smoothie goes for the taste and color of bright pink strawberry milk; ditch the sugar-syrup and grab a glass of the real thing!

MAKES 2 PINTS

⅛ cup dried hibiscus flower petals
2 cups hot water
⅓ cup raw cashews
1½ cups frozen strawberries
½ frozen banana
6 Medjool dates
2 Tbsp hemp seeds
½ tsp natural strawberry flavoring (optional)

Soak the hibiscus flower petals in the hot water for at least 10 minutes, then add to the blender. You can choose to strain out the flowers through a small mesh strainer, or leave them in for added nutrition. You can also add the flowers to the hot water the night before and let it steep, covered, overnight so the water will be cool by morning.

Blend the cashews and water for 2 minutes with a high-speed blender, then combine the remaining ingredients and blend for several minutes until smooth.

Note: You can order organic dried hibiscus flowers online; hibiscus flowers are one of the highest sources of antioxidants you can find!

Zucchini Bread Smoothie

This is an offbeat fruit smoothie—zucchini is technically a fruit, after all!

MAKES 2 PINTS

⅓ cup raw walnuts
¼ cup rolled oats
1 Tbsp flax seeds
2 cups water
1 frozen banana
1 cup shredded zucchini or 1 small zucchini
¼ cup raisins
1 tsp ground cinnamon
1 ½ tsp vanilla extract
1 tsp Nutiva Buttery Coconut Spread
¼ tsp ground nutmeg
¼ tsp powdered ginger
⅛ tsp sea salt

Blend the walnuts, oats, and flax seeds with the water for 2 minutes, then add the remaining ingredients and blend for an additional 2 minutes until smooth.

Note: Adding uncooked oats to smoothies make them more filling, and they are also one of the most nutrient-dense foods you can eat!

Cranberry Harvest Smoothie

This is one of my favorite smoothies; it's autumn in a glass!

MAKES 2 PINTS

⅓ cup raw almonds
2 cups water
1½ cups frozen cranberries
1 frozen banana
1 apple, cored and sliced
4 Medjool dates
1 Tbsp flax seeds
1 tsp powdered ginger, or 1" sliced ginger
½ tsp ground cinnamon
⅛ tsp ground nutmeg
⅛ tsp ground cloves

Blend the almonds and water together for 1 minute. Add the remaining ingredients and blend until smooth.

Note: Cranberries aren't just for Thanksgiving; enjoy cranberries throughout the year by buying them frozen. Cranberries are little red nutritional powerhouses!

Pumpkin Pie Smoothie

For those who worship the pumpkin spice, this smoothie is for you!

MAKES 2 PINTS

⅓ cup raw pecans
2 cups water
1 cup cooked pumpkin, or half a 14 oz. can pumpkin puree
1 frozen banana
4 Medjool dates
1 Tbsp flax seeds
2 tsp ground cinnamon
1½ tsp vanilla extract
½ tsp powdered ginger, or 1" fresh ginger
¼ tsp ground allspice
⅛ tsp ground cloves
2 squares graham cracker, crushed

Blend the pecans and water together for 1 minute, then add the remaining ingredients and blend 2 minutes until smooth. Mix in the crushed graham cracker before serving.

Note: If using fresh pumpkin, cube and cook the pumpkin, then freeze and use it whenever you want for this smoothie.

Strawberry Cheesecake Smoothie

Strawberry, blueberry, or cherry cheesecake—it's up to you! Forget the tubs of cream cheese, and raise a glass of cheesecake smoothie to your health!

MAKES 2 PINTS

⅓ cup raw cashews
2 cups water
1½ cups fresh strawberries (or blueberries or cherries)
½ frozen banana
Zest of ½ lemon
Juice of ½ lemon
3 Medjool dates
1 Tbsp chia seeds
¼ tsp natural strawberry flavoring (optional)
⅛ tsp sea salt
2 squares graham cracker, crushed

Blend the cashews and water for 1 minute. Add the remaining ingredients and blend for several minutes until completely smooth. Crumble the graham cracker and sprinkle over the smoothie in a glass, or use a spoon and mix it in.

Note: Zest the lemon before cutting and juicing it; it's much easier to zest before you juice it than after!

Sweet Potato Pie Smoothie

Sweet potatoes are so delicious and healthy, I'm always looking for excuses to add more to the menu, and this smoothie is a perfect opportunity!

MAKES 2 PINTS

⅓ cup raw pecans
2 cups water
1 medium cooked sweet potato, peeled, or 1 cup cubed
1 frozen banana
1" fresh ginger, or ¼" powdered ginger
2 Medjool dates
1 Tbsp flax seeds
1 tsp vanilla extract
1 tsp pumpkin pie spice
¼ tsp sea salt

Blend the pecans and water for 1 minute, then add the remaining ingredients and blend until smooth.

Note: I like to boil cubes of sweet potato and freeze them so that I have them on hand when I need them.

Black Forest Smoothie

The taste of chocolate and cherries together is a winning combination!

MAKES 2 PINTS

⅓ cup raw almonds
¼ cup rolled oats
2 cups water
½ frozen banana
1½ cups frozen cherries
4 Medjool dates
3 Tbsp cacao powder
1 Tbsp chia seeds
1 tsp vanilla extract
½ tsp almond extract
¼ tsp espresso powder

Blend the almonds and water together for 1 minute, then add remaining ingredients and blend for several minutes until completely smooth.

Note: I prefer using frozen cherries for this smoothie; they're quicker than pitting fresh cherries, and are more consistent (fresh cherries can spoil quickly).

Grasshopper Pie Smoothie

One of the many benefits of being vegan is that it's an easy excuse not to jump on the eating-insects-as-protein bandwagon—"Sorry, that's not vegan!" There are plenty of plant-based sources of protein, rest assured. This smoothie is quite free of grasshoppers and is full of minty goodness!

MAKES 2 PINTS

¼ cup raw almonds
¼ cup rolled oats
2 cups water
1 frozen banana
1 cup packed fresh or frozen spinach
¼ cup fresh mint leaves
3 Medjool dates
3 Tbsp cacao powder
1 Tbsp flax seeds
1 tsp vanilla extract
½ tsp peppermint extract
¼ tsp espresso powder
2 squares graham cracker, crushed

Blend the almonds and water together for 1 minute, then add the remaining ingredients and blend until smooth. Crumble the graham cracker over the smoothie in a glass.

Note: Mint is a delicious and nutritious herb, and the best way to maximize that nutrition is to use it fresh.

Truth be told, the color of this smoothie comes out somewhere between green and brown, not the most appetizing smoothie in the cookbook to look at, granted. But it tastes delicious and is very healthy. So if you need to fool your eyes to enjoy this smoothie, then skip the Mason jar and try another cup that isn't transparent. . . .

Blackberry Cobbler Smoothie

Blackberries are one of nature's perfect packages—little morsels of sweet and tart goodness, and loaded with nutrition!

MAKES 2 PINTS

⅛ cup dried butterfly pea flower petals (optional, for color)
2 cups hot water
¼ cup raw walnuts
⅓ cup rolled oats
½ frozen banana
1½ cups frozen blackberries
4 Medjool dates
1 Tbsp hemp seeds
½ tsp ground cinnamon
½ tsp vanilla extract
½ tsp Nutiva Coconut Buttery Spread
⅛ tsp sea salt

Steep the flowers in hot water for 5 minutes, then add the flowers/water mixture to the blender with the walnuts and oats, and blend for 1 minute. Add the remaining ingredients and blend for several minutes until completely smooth.

Note: You can buy dried butterfly pea flowers online; they give this smoothie a strong blue color and are a great source of antioxidants.

If fresh blackberries aren't available year round in your area, when they're in season stock up the freezer and use them throughout the rest of the year!

Chocolate Peanut Butter Smoothie

It's hard to go wrong with the taste of chocolate and peanut butter. Here, we put a healthy twist on a perfect combination!

MAKES 2 PINTS

¼ cup rolled oats
⅓ cup roasted, unsalted peanuts
2 cups water
1½ frozen bananas
½ medium cooked sweet potato, or ½ cup cooked sweet potato
3 Medjool dates
3 Tbsp cacao powder
1 Tbsp flax seeds
2 tsp maca powder (optional)
1 tsp vanilla extract
¼ tsp espresso powder
¼ tsp sea salt

Blend the oats, peanuts, and water for 1 minute, then add the remaining ingredients and blend until smooth.

Note: Maca powder gives this smoothie a malted flavoring, and it's also nutrient-rich. You can find maca powder in health food stores or online.

Very Grape Smoothie

This smoothie will help make you as strong as a giant ape! It reminds me of the taste of the grape-flavored drinks I had as a kid, but now it's healthy and nutritious (shh . . . don't tell the kids!).

MAKES 2 PINTS

⅓ cup rolled oats
2 cups water
1 ½ cups seedless red grapes
½ frozen banana
¼ cup frozen blueberries
3 Medjool dates
1 tsp dried pomegranate seeds
Several drops natural grape flavoring (optional)

Blend the oats and water together for 1 minute, then add the remaining ingredients. Blend on high for several minutes to blend the grape skins as well as possible.

Note: Grapes give this smoothie a unique texture. Since whole grapes are almost like jelly inside their skins, they give this smoothie a gel-like consistency.

Hibiscus Peach Ginger Smoothie

This was my first smoothie recipe that I tried using dried flowers; what a great addition the hibiscus makes!

MAKES 2 PINTS

¼ cup dried hibiscus flower petals
2 cups hot water
⅓ cup raw pecans
1 frozen banana
1 cup frozen peaches
4 Medjool dates
1 Tbsp hemp seeds
½" fresh ginger, or ¼" powdered ginger
¼ tsp ground cinnamon

Soak the hibiscus flowers in hot water (it can be hot from the tap; it doesn't have to be boiling) for at least 5 minutes, then add the mixture to the blender and blend with the pecans for several minutes. Add the remaining ingredients and blend for several more minutes.

Note: When using dried flowers in smoothies like hibiscus, steep them in hot water first before blending them in; don't throw any of that nutrition away! Alternatively, you could use a small mesh strainer to strain out the hibiscus flowers instead of adding them to the blender.

Kiwi Elegance Green Smoothie

Elegant was the first thing that came to mind when I first tasted this smoothie—the combination of fruit, spinach, and macadamia nuts create a complex flavor very different from traditional green smoothies!

MAKES 2 PINTS

¼ cup raw macadamia nuts
2 cups water
½ frozen banana
2 kiwifruits, core the ends but leave the peels on
1 cup frozen strawberries
1 cup packed fresh or frozen spinach
3 Medjool dates
1 Tbsp chia seeds
¼ tsp ground cinnamon

Blend the macadamia nuts and the water for 2 minutes. Add the remaining ingredients and blend for several minutes.

Note: Eating the fuzzy skin of kiwifruit triples their fiber over eating just the flesh of the fruit, plus the skins are loaded with nutrients, so leave those peels on!

Peanut Butter Cookie Smoothie

This smoothie is liquid gold—so good, just like a peanut butter cookie but without the butter, sugar, and eggs. What kind of food alchemy is this?

MAKES 2 PINTS

¼ cup roasted, unsalted peanuts
¼ cup rolled oats
2 cups water
1 frozen banana
6 Medjool dates
2 Tbsp powdered peanut butter
1 tsp Nutiva Coconut Buttery Spread
1 Tbsp hemp seeds
½ tsp vanilla extract
¼ tsp sea salt

Blend the peanuts, oats, and water in a high-speed blender until smooth. Add the remaining ingredients and continue to blend until smooth. Pour into a glass, and sprinkle extra peanut butter powder on top.

Lemon-Lime Basil Smoothie

To anyone who's tried basil lemonade, congratulations on taking a leap of faith and trying two flavor combinations that you wouldn't necessarily put together: lemons and basil. For everyone else, I encourage you to take the leap!

MAKES 2 PINTS

⅓ cup raw almonds
2 cups water
1 frozen banana
1 cup frozen mango chunks
1 cup frozen spinach
½ cup chopped basil
Juice of 1 lemon
Juice of 1 lime
4 Medjool dates
1 Tbsp hemp seeds

Blend the almonds and water in a high-speed blender until smooth, then add the remaining ingredients and blend until well combined.

Gingerbread Smoothie

The spices and fresh ginger combine here to make a sweet breakfast treat that lets you enjoy the taste of gingerbread any time of year.

MAKES 2 PINTS

¼ cup raw almonds
¼ cup rolled oats
2 cups water
1 frozen banana
1 medium carrot
½" fresh ginger
3 Medjool dates
1 Tbsp blackstrap molasses
1 Tbsp flax seeds
1 tsp vanilla extract
½ tsp ground cinnamon
¼ tsp ground nutmeg
¼ tsp ground allspice

Add the almonds, rolled oats, and water to a high-speed blender and blend for 1 minute. Add the remaining ingredients and blend several minutes until completely smooth.

Strawberry Rhubarb Crisp Smoothie

Don't be scared by the raw rhubarb; this sweet smoothie gives you the delicious taste of strawberry rhubarb crisp but without all the baking and the unhealthy ingredients.

MAKES 2 PINTS

2 stalks rhubarb (about 1 cup chopped)
2 cups water
⅓ cup rolled oats
¼ cup raw pecans
1½ cups frozen strawberries
6 Medjool dates
1 Tbsp flax seeds
1 Tbsp blackstrap molasses
1 tsp vanilla extract
1 tsp Nutiva Coconut Buttery Spread
½ tsp ground cinnamon
¼ tsp sea salt

Using a high-power blender, blend the rhubarb with the water for 2 minutes. If you're using a standard blender, blend for several minutes and pour through a strainer or cheesecloth to remove the rhubarb pulp. Blend the remaining ingredients for several minutes until smooth.

Note: Rhubarb is only in season for several weeks in my area, and usually friends who have rhubarb are more than happy to give it away since it grows in such abundance! I take home stalks of rhubarb and chop them into 1" pieces, and freeze them in a resealable bag to use them for months to come.

Harmony Fennel Smoothie

Fresh fennel has a strong and unique flavor similar to licorice, so you might worry that it would overpower the taste of everything else in a smoothie. In this heart-healthy creamy smoothie, we get fennel to play nice and be a part of the flavor conversation without dominating it!

MAKES 2 PINTS

2 cups coconut water
½ bulb of fennel, chopped
⅓ cup raw cashews
1 cup frozen mango chunks
1 apple, cored and sliced
1" fresh ginger
4 Medjool dates
Juice of ½ lemon
1 Tbsp hemp seeds

In a high-powered blender, combine the coconut water, fennel, cashews, and mango, and blend several minutes until completely smooth. Add the remaining ingredients and continue to blend several minutes until all the ingredients are well combined.

Note: There are only a handful of smoothie recipes in this book that call for coconut water; it can get expensive and isn't always the easiest to find at the grocery store. Unrefrigerated boxed coconut water that can last up to six months on the shelf is usually the most convenient way kind to buy. If you want to use fresh coconut water, a fresh young coconut (if you can find it) is a real treat; usually coconut water in the store is from young coconuts rather than the hard-shelled brown mature coconuts that have to be cracked open.

Summer Blush Fruit Smoothie

This rosy smoothie is full of fresh summer fruit to make you feel as radiant as the sun!

MAKES 2 PINTS

⅓ cup raw almonds
2 cups water or hibiscus tea
1 cup raspberries
1 navel orange, peeled
1 medium carrot
½ frozen banana
3 Medjool dates
1 Tbsp flax seeds

Add the almonds and water (or tea) to a high-speed blender, and blend until smooth. Add the remaining ingredients and continue to blend several minutes more until well combined.

Mild-Mannered Mint Green Smoothie

I have to admit that I'm not a big fan of the green smoothie recipes I typically see online, loaded with kale and different veggies. I've made many of the recipes to try them, hoping maybe there is a flavor combination that makes liquid kale taste good, but alas, my taste buds aren't impressed. The Kiwi Elegance Smoothie is also a delicious and healthy green smoothie, but I wanted something with lots of greens that was tasty but also subtler in flavor, so please enjoy my Mild-Mannered Mint Green Smoothie!

MAKES 2 PINTS

⅓ cup raw almonds
2 cups water
1 cup green grapes
2 Persian cucumbers, peeled and roughly chopped
½ frozen banana
¼ cup fresh mint
3 Medjool dates
1 Tbsp hemp seeds
½ tsp vanilla extract

Combine the almonds and water in a high-speed blender and blend until smooth. Add the remaining ingredients and blend for several minutes until well combined.

Peanut Butter and Jelly Smoothie

PB and J sandwiches have always been my favorite, and this smoothie is a whole-food spin on my old favorite.

MAKES 2 PINTS

½ cup roasted, unsalted peanuts
2 cups water
1 frozen banana
1½ cups black, red, or concord grapes, seedless
4 Medjool dates
1 Tbsp hemp seeds
⅛ tsp sea salt

Add the peanuts and water to a high-speed blender, and blend several minutes until completely smooth. Add the remaining ingredients and blend several more minutes.

Apps and Sides

Salads and Dressings

Once at a weeklong training workshop, the host generously provided my team with lunch from the local deli, but the only vegan option was a garden salad: iceberg lettuce, tomatoes that were probably picked six months earlier, a few shreds of carrot and purple cabbage, and oil and vinegar. Two days in, one of my classmates asked me, "How do you eat like that every day? That must be so *boring*." So I had to assure my classmate that as a vegan I don't, in fact, eat rabbit food every day—while not offending my host about the free lunches.

I don't mind eating salads; there are plenty of veggies and toppings to choose from, but even so, eating a lot of salad can get boring fast. For me, the best way to keep things interesting is to switch up my salad dressings by using these delicious recipes!

How do you make salad dressings healthier? Low- or fat-free dressings you find in the stores take out the oil, increase the sugar, and use thickening agents that make it more slimy than creamy. I can help you make creamy and delicious salad dressings without using oil, but there's an important tradeoff: it's not going to last more than a week in the refrigerator. You know that bottle of salad dressing in your fridge that's been there for months? The oil plus the added preservatives keep that salad dressing around a lot longer than it would last naturally. The good news is that you can always freeze these salad dressings if you don't use them up within a week.

My secret to replacing oil in salad dressings is to substitute cashews. Cashews give these dressings the same creamy texture as oil but with only a fifth of the fat and a fifth of the calories. You won't see food companies use this substitute because it won't last for weeks or months, and nobody expects to find salad dressing in the freezer aisle. Plus, for some reason people still think that olive oil is a "heart-healthy" fat. Besides the fact that cashews only have a small fraction of the fat as olive oil, your body can process fat from nuts easily, whereas olive oil is an extremely calorie-dense food with no fiber or nutrition—just empty calories.

Of course, salads are not just lettuce and chopped vegetables, and you'll find plenty of other salad recipes here too. Any one of these recipes will give you lunch for days, either with some soup, on its own with crackers or veggies, or as a sandwich or wrap. Rabbit food. Hmpf!

Salads and Dressings as a System

You can store these salad dressings in 1-cup Mason jars and freeze what you're not going to use within several days.

Many of the salads in this chapter can be served several ways: in a sandwich, in a wrap, with crackers, or on their own. You can combine salad fillings like tabbouleh and hummus with fresh veggies, and roll them into wraps, then store them wrapped up for lunches for the week. One tip for making wraps easier to roll: wet each side and microwave for 20–30 seconds, which makes them more pliable.

Salads and Dressings

Toasted Coconut and Jicama Salad

Is this a salad or a dessert? One of the benefits of whole-food, plant-based eating is that salads can be sweet and delicious, and desserts can be healthy and nutritious. So dessert for lunch? Sure! Salad for dessert? You bet! It's a mixed-up world.

MAKES 3½ CUPS

Coconut meat of ½ fresh coconut, shredded, or 1½ cup shredded
    dried coconut, unsweetened
½ jicama, peeled and shredded
½ cup dried or fresh cranberries
½ cup chopped raw pecans
2 Tbsp coconut water
1 Tbsp maple syrup
½ tsp ground nutmeg
½ tsp sea salt

Preheat oven to 325°F. Shred coconut and jicama, then combine on a rimmed baking sheet and cook for several minutes. Remove and stir, and return to oven for several more minutes. Continue to remove, stir, and bake for a few minutes at a time until the coconut shreds turn light brown. Once the shreds are cooked, combine in a metal mixing bowl with the remaining ingredients, and serve.

Note: If you don't drink coconut water regularly, it can be helpful to pour a container of coconut water into an ice cube tray and freeze it, then store the cubes in a freezer bag to use when you need it for recipes like this.

ChickSea Salad

Vegan recipes like this one are typically meant to be mock tuna salads, but that sets up false expectations. Personally, I never really liked tuna—it reminded me too much of cat food. Fortunately, this recipe (in my opinion) tastes much better than tuna salad, so instead of calling it a mock tuna salad, I like to celebrate it as its own, unique thing. If you want to give it a sea flavor, feel free to throw in some dulse flakes!

MAKES 2½ CUPS

1½ cups cooked chickpeas
⅓ cup Eggless Mayo (see **Odds and Ends**)
¼ cup red onion, finely chopped
2 stalks celery, finely chopped
¼ cup dill pickle, finely chopped
Juice of ½ lemon
½ Tbsp nutritional yeast
1 Tbsp prepared yellow mustard
1 Tbsp tamari
1 tsp dried dill
1 tsp dulse flakes
½ tsp garlic powder
½ tsp sea salt

Mash the chickpeas with a potato masher until the beans are broken up; you don't want to mash them until they're smooth. Mix in the remaining ingredients and stir until well combined.

Note: Serve on bread with sprouts, sliced tomato, cucumber, sliced avocado, lettuce, et cetera, or eat with crackers.

Uncanny Valley Tofu Salad

When animation is drawn to be more realistic than cartoonish, it can be eerie to watch and is referred to as the "uncanny valley." The use of black salt brings this tofu salad into the culinary uncanny valley with its sulfur flavor, and the texture of the crumbled tofu makes it eerily similar to egg salad. It's always fun to watch people in my cooking classes try this recipe, because they saw what ingredients were used yet it tastes so similar to egg salad.

MAKES 2½ CUPS

One 15 oz. block of firm tofu
⅓ cup Eggless Mayo (see **Odds and Ends**)
½ yellow onion, finely diced
2 stalks celery, diced
1 Tbsp yellow mustard
1 tsp black sea salt
½ tsp garlic powder
½ tsp turmeric powder
½ tsp paprika

In a large mixing bowl, mash the tofu with a potato masher until crumbled, then mix in the remaining ingredients.

Note: Black salt can be found in natural food stores, Indian markets, or online. Black salt has a distinct sulfur taste that makes all the difference in this recipe, so although it may be a specialty item, I recommend tracking it down for recipes like this!

Black Bean and Roasted Corn Salsa

Warning: this salsa will disappear quickly at parties! It's hard to stop once you dip a chip into this salsa, but since it's loaded with fresh, whole-food ingredients, you don't need to!

MAKES 6 CUPS

3 cups frozen corn
¼ tsp liquid smoke
1 Tbsp tamari
1 large tomato, chopped
1½ cups cooked black beans
1 green pepper, finely chopped
¼ cup red onion, finely chopped
Juice of 1 lime
1 Tbsp apple cider vinegar
1 Tbsp olive oil, optional
½ cup fresh cilantro, chopped
½ tsp sea salt
¼ tsp ground chipotle pepper
¼ tsp ground cumin
¼ tsp garlic powder

In a non-stick frying pan on medium heat, combine the corn, liquid smoke, and tamari, and continue to stir until the corn is roasted. Add the corn to a large mixing bowl with the remaining ingredients, stir well, and serve.

Hummus

This hummus recipe really has me spoiled; once you try fresh hummus it's hard to have store-bought! I've tried many flavors of hummus, but this simple, traditional hummus remains my favorite.

MAKES 2½ CUPS

1½ cups cooked chickpeas
½ cup tahini
Juice of 1 lemon
1 clove garlic
1 tsp ground cumin
½ tsp sea salt
½ cup water

Add all ingredients to a food processor and blend until smooth. Add more water as necessary for a thinner consistency.

Note: To make hummus with the same smooth consistency of store-bought hummus, use a high-speed blender instead of a food processor.

Tabbouleh

This recipe has just the right combination of fresh parsley, mint, bulgur, and tomato for my taste buds. Like many of the recipes in this book, if you've only ever had store-bought tabbouleh, there is no comparison to fresh tabbouleh!

MAKES 3 CUPS

2 bunches flat leaf parsley
1 cup fresh mint
½ yellow onion
½ cup uncooked bulgur
1 tomato, well chopped
1 Tbsp olive oil
Juice of 1 lemon
1 tsp sea salt

Add the parsley, mint and onion to a food processor with an "S" blade and process until it's finely chopped, stopping to scrape down the sides several times.

Boil 1 cup of water and then add the bulgur. Remove from heat and cover, and let it sit for 15 minutes.

Add the bulgur, the parsley/mint/onion mixture and diced tomatoes into a mixing bowl, add the olive oil, lemon juice, and salt, and mix well.

Note: Although it's tempting to grab a spoon and eat this tabbouleh straight, I like to eat it with crackers, slices of pita bread, or rolled in a pita as a wrap.

This is one of only a few recipes in this cookbook that calls for olive oil. Though usually much more olive oil is used in making tabbouleh, I find that 1 tablespoon is enough to coat the tabbouleh so that it doesn't get dry. I've tried making this recipe in different ways without the olive oil and it falls short, so here, where I feel like a little makes a big difference, I will use it.

Sesame Noodle Salad

*This Asian-inspired noodle salad makes a delicious and hearty lunch!
Split up a batch into smaller containers, and you'll have to-go lunches
for days!*

MAKES 4 CUPS

FOR THE SALAD:
⅓ lb. uncooked spaghetti noodles or linguini
1 medium carrot, peeled and cut into 1" matchsticks
2 Persian cucumbers, unpeeled and diced
1 red bell pepper, diced
½ cup shredded purple cabbage

FOR THE SAUCE:
1 Tbsp toasted sesame oil (or tahini)
2 Tbsp apple cider vinegar
2 Tbsp tamari
2 Tbsp agave nectar
1 tsp garlic powder
1 tsp powered ginger
½ tsp sriracha

TOPPINGS:
¼ cup chopped roasted peanuts, unsalted
¼ cup fresh cilantro, chopped
2 scallions, minced
2 Tbsp sesame seeds

Cook the noodles according to the directions on the package,
then add to a large mixing bowl with the carrots, cucumbers,

and bell pepper. Mix together until well combined. Combine the sauce ingredients in a bowl and whisk together, then pour over the salad. Use tongs to add the salad to individual bowls, then add the toppings and serve.

Note: Store-bought sesame noodle salads often use buckwheat soba noodles, which is more authentic, but I prefer the texture of spaghetti to cold soba noodles, so ultimately it's a matter of your personal taste. Here we use toasted sesame oil for flavoring, not as a base. Toasted sesame oil has a rich taste that isn't easily substituted, but you can use tahini instead if you prefer to avoid even small amounts of added oil.

Thai Larb Salad

Traditionally, Thai Larb is a meat salad made with minced pork or chicken and sticky rice. Here we'll ditch the meat and keep the lime juice and herbs, which is what really gives this dish its signature flavor.

MAKES 3 CUPS

One 8 oz. package tempeh, cubed
1 package shiitake mushrooms
1 medium shallot, chopped
2 scallions, chopped
Juice of 1 lime
3 Tbsp tamari
1 tsp dulse flakes
1 tsp sriracha
1 tsp agave nectar
1" slice ginger, grated
¼ cup fresh mint
¼ cup fresh cilantro
¼ cup basil (optional)
½ stalk lemongrass
10–12 butter lettuce or romaine lettuce leaves
Chopped roasted peanuts, unsalted for topping

Add the tempeh, mushrooms, shallots, and scallions to a food processor and blend the ingredients until the tempeh is chopped into small pieces.

Add the contents of the food processor to a large saucepan or skillet along with the lime juice, tamari, dulse flakes, sriracha, grated ginger, and agave nectar, and stir constantly over medium heat until the mushrooms are cooked. While the tempeh mixture is cooking, add the mint, cilantro, basil (if using), and lemongrass to the food processor and pulse several times until the herbs are chopped well. Add the herbs to the pan and cook for an additional minute, then spoon the mixture into leaves of lettuce to serve.

Som Tum Papaya Salad

This Thai papaya salad is mixture of sweet and tangy, another deli-cious way to get in your fruits and veggies!

MAKES 3½ CUPS

1 small green papaya
3 large carrots, peeled
1 cup cherry tomatoes, sliced in halves
Juice of 2 limes
2 Tbsp tamari
2 Tbsp coarsely chopped roasted peanuts, unsalted
1 Tbsp agave nectar
1 tsp garlic powder
½ tsp dulse flakes
¼ tsp chili powder
¼ tsp sea salt

Use a mandoline to cut the papaya and carrots into ¼" julienne strips, or cut with a chopping knife. The papaya is traditionally pounded in a clay mortar and pestle until it's softened, but that can be quite a workout! My solution is to use a stand mixer with a paddle beater, and let the mixer do the work for me, or if you don't have the clay mortar or stand mixer, use a potato masher to beat the papaya in a mixing bowl. Once the papaya is softened, add the remaining ingredients and serve.

Note: If you can't find green papaya in the supermarket (you can often find them in Asian and Indian markets), you can substitute with red papaya.

Israeli Salad

You don't need lettuce to make a salad! These fresh veggies come together for a tangy salad that is perfect on their own!

MAKES 4 CUPS

8 Persian cucumbers, unpeeled and diced
4 fresh ripe Roma tomatoes, seeded and diced
⅓ cup minced yellow onion
½ cup minced flat leaf parsley
3 Tbsp chopped fresh dill
1 Tbsp olive oil
3 Tbsp lemon juice
½ tsp sea salt

Combine all ingredients and mix well.

Coleslaw of Many Colors

This salad is as colorful as it is delicious!

MAKES 5 CUPS

1½ cups cabbage green, shredded
1½ cups purple cabbage, shredded
1 medium carrot, diced
½ green bell pepper, diced
½ red bell pepper, diced
½ yellow bell pepper, diced
½ cup raw pecans, chopped
3 scallions, chopped
⅔ cup Eggless Mayo (see **Odds and Ends**)
1 Tbsp apple cider vinegar
1 Tbsp agave nectar
2 tsp caraway seeds, whole (or ground, optional)
1 tsp sea salt

Combine all ingredients in a large mixing bowl and stir until combined, then serve. I prefer to grind the caraway seeds to a powder for this recipe so that there is a more consistent caraway taste in each bite.

Asian Fusion Salad

This Asian salad is a combination of Chinese and Indian influences. It's a Chinese salad with a sweet and tangy sauce over Napa cabbage, and I added some Madras curry powder with Indian crunchy noodles to top it off. This delicious salad doesn't last long in my house!

MAKES 4 CUPS

FOR THE SALAD:
½ small head Napa cabbage, chopped
1 medium carrot, shredded
½ red bell pepper, diced
¼ cup fresh cilantro, chopped
½ block extra-firm tofu, cubed

FOR THE SAUCE:
2 Tbsp apple cider vinegar
2 Tbsp tamari
1 Tbsp tahini
1 Tbsp toasted sesame oil
1 Tbsp agave nectar
1 tsp Madras Curry Powder (see **Odds and Ends**)
¼ tsp chili powder

TOPPINGS:
Bhujia (bean flour noodles) or uncooked ramen noodles
Sesame seeds

Chop the salad ingredients and combine in a large mixing bowl. In a small bowl, combine the sauce ingredients and whisk together, then pour the sauce over the salad. Use a large spoon to mix the sauce into the salad. Before serving, top with Bhujia (or uncooked ramen noodles) and sesame seeds.

Note: The crunchy noodles add a great texture to the salad; make sure to add them as a topping right before serving so they stay crunchy. You can find Bhujia noodles in Indian markets or order them online, or you can use uncooked ramen noodles (which are already cooked and dehydrated, so they're safe to eat uncooked out of the package).

Native Wild Rice Salad

Grass has never tasted so good! (Wild rice is technically a type of grass seed, not a grain.)

MAKES 5 CUPS

FOR THE SALAD:
1 cup uncooked wild rice
4 cups water
1 tsp Better Than Bouillon, Vegetable flavor
1 cup chopped raw pecans
1 cup dried cranberries
1 cup frozen corn
Zest of 1 navel orange
2 scallions, chopped

FOR THE DRESSING:
⅓ cup apple cider vinegar
3 Medjool dates
¼ cup raw cashews
¼ cup leftover liquid from cooked rice
Juice of 1 navel orange

Cook the rice until tender, then drain and set aside the excess water. Add the remaining ingredients for the salad and mix to combine. Add the ingredients for the dressing to a high-speed blender and blend until smooth. Add the dressing to the salad and toss to combine, then serve.

Ocean House Salad

I've tried a few different vegan "lobster" rolls at restaurants and, while I really liked the flavor combinations and textures, I thought it was bizarre to call them lobster rolls. They were nothing like lobster (fortunately, as I never liked the taste of lobster), and I felt like they would stand well on their own as their own thing. So, like other kinds of mayo-based salads, this salad is great as a sandwich or on a roll. And leave the lobsters in the ocean (seriously, lobsters are like the spiders of the ocean floor; even if you like the taste of lobster why would you eat that? Okay, rant done).

MAKES 3½ CUPS

One 14 oz. can artichoke hearts
One 14 oz. can organic hearts of palm
½ cup Eggless Mayo (see **Odds and Ends**)
2 stalks celery, diced
1 shallot, diced
1 Tbsp lemon juice
1 tsp Old Bay Seasoning
1 tsp dried dill
1 tsp sea salt
1 tsp dulse flakes
1 tsp sriracha

Rinse the artichoke hearts and hearts of palm first, then add them to a food processor and pulse until they're chopped into smaller pieces, but not pureed. Transfer to a large mixing bowl, add the remaining ingredients, and stir until well combined.

Seaweed Salad

I love seaweed salad at Japanese restaurants and I wanted to recreate the same tastes at home, but I found it hard to find the right kind of seaweed. Wakame might not be the same as what you'd find at the restaurants, but it's loaded with vitamins and nutrients and is a mild type of seaweed.

MAKES 2 CUPS

FOR THE SALAD:
¼ cup dried wakame seaweed (from Maine)
2 Persian cucumbers, unpeeled

FOR THE DRESSING:
3 Tbsp tamari
3 Tbsp apple cider vinegar
1 Tbsp agave nectar
1 Tbsp toasted sesame oil
½ tsp powdered ginger

TOPPING:
1 Tbs. sesame seeds

Soak the wakame in a bowl for 10 minutes, then strain and press the water out as much as possible. Cut the cucumbers into small matchstick strips and lay out on a plate, then add the seaweed. Pour dressing over the wakame, and sprinkle with sesame seeds.

Note: There is a lot of debate in the health world about the safety of eating seaweed from Japan due to high levels of arsenic, so I recommend looking for seaweed from the coast of Maine.

Arame Salad over Rice

Seaweed can be a great source of healthy nutrients, but for me a little goes a long way. Arame is a mild-tasting seaweed that adds a nice accent without overpowering the dish!

MAKES 5½ CUPS

Half a 15 oz. block extra-firm tofu

1 tsp turmeric powder

1 tsp toasted sesame oil

½ tsp sea salt

2 cups cooked short-grain brown rice

2 dried shiitake mushroom caps, cut into ¼" wide strips

1 Tbsp agave nectar

1 Tbsp apple cider vinegar

1 Tbsp tamari

1 cup dried arame seaweed

1 large carrot, cut into 2" julienne strips

½ cup shelled edamame (frozen is fine)

2 Tbsp mirin

2 Tbsp tamari

½ Tbsp agave nectar

½ Tbsp toasted sesame oil

1 Tbsp sake

1 tsp ground black pepper

Preheat the oven to 400° F. Cut the tofu into ¼" slabs; you should be able to get about 5 from a half block of tofu. In a mixing bowl, combine the turmeric, sesame oil, and salt, then coat each slab of tofu in the mixture and place on a silicone baking mat or non-stick baking sheet, and cook for 10 minutes.

Remove from the oven, flip the tofu over, and cook for an additional 10 minutes.

Cook the brown rice with the shiitake mushroom strips, and when the rice is fully cooked, add the agave, apple cider vinegar, and tamari.

Soak the arame for 10 minutes in a separate bowl. Meanwhile, in a large saucepan, add the carrots, edamame, drained arame, and the remaining ingredients. Slice the cooked tofu into ¼" strips and add to the saucepan, and cook on medium for 10 minutes, stirring regularly.

Serve the seaweed mixture over the rice.

Dressing of the Goddesses

Goddess Dressing has been a divine indulgence for me. I love the taste, but as with most salad dressings there's so much fat that goes with the flavor. With this recipe and the ones that follow, I've cut out the oil and kept the great taste!

MAKES 1½ CUPS

¼ cup raw cashews
¼ cup water
½ cup tahini
¼ cup apple cider vinegar
2 Tbsp tamari
2 Tbsp lemon juice
2 cloves garlic
1 tsp sea salt
3 Tbsp fresh parsley, finely chopped
2 Tbsp chives, finely chopped

Blend the first eight ingredients in a high-speed blender, pour into a dressing bottle, and add the parsley and chives. Shake well before serving.

Shiitake Mushroom Dressing

The toasted sesame oil and mushrooms gives this dressing a rich flavor that dresses up a garden salad any time.

MAKES 2 CUPS

1 cup boiling water
2 dried shiitake mushroom caps
½ cup raw cashews
⅓ cup apple cider vinegar
3 Tbsp tamari
2 tsp toasted sesame oil
2 tsp sesame seeds

Soak dried mushrooms in boiling water for 10 minutes, then drain and save the soaking water. Use ½ cup of the soaking water to blend with the cashews, apple cider vinegar, tamari, and sesame oil until smooth. Use a hand chopper to cut the cooked mushrooms into small pieces, or chop with a knife. In a small skillet, toast the sesame seeds over medium heat and stir frequently until the seeds are browned. Combine the blender ingredients, mushroom pieces, and sesame seeds in a dressing bottle and shake until combined. Add more of the mushroom soaking water for thinner consistency if desired.

French Dressing

Using fresh tomatoes in this French dressing recipe makes all the difference. It's so much more flavorful than what you'll find in the supermarket, you'll ditch the store-bought bottle forever!

MAKES 2½ CUPS

1 cup chopped tomatoes
8 Medjool dates
½ cup apple cider vinegar
⅓ cup raw cashews
¼ cup water
1 medium shallot
1 Tbsp lemon juice
1 tsp celery salt
½ tsp dried mustard
½ tsp celery seed
¼ tsp ground black pepper

Combine all ingredients in a high-speed blender and blend until completely smooth. Pour into a small saucepan and simmer for 10 minutes to cook the tomatoes, then bottle the sauce and let it cool first before using. Add more water to thin as needed.

Creamy Italian Dressing

Normally drenched in oil, this recipe reimagines a creamy dressing with the great taste of Italian seasonings but without all the oil!

MAKES 1½ CUPS

½–1 cup water
½ cup raw cashews
2 pitted green olives
¼ cup apple cider vinegar
1 Tbsp nutritional yeast
1 Tbsp dried Italian seasonings
1 tsp garlic powder
1 tsp sea salt

Blend the water, cashews, olive, and apple cider vinegar in a high-speed blender until smooth, then pour into a dressing bottle with the remaining ingredients and shake well until combined.

Note: It can be more convenient to buy a jar of Italian seasoning for this recipe, but if you prefer to buy the dried herbs individually instead, you would need equal parts basil, oregano, rosemary, thyme, and marjoram.

Sun Gold Dressing

This dressing recipe is one of my favorite ways to make a garden salad disappear quickly!

MAKES 1½ CUPS

½ cup nutritional yeast
½–1 cup water
¼ cup raw cashews
2 Tbsp apple cider vinegar
1 tsp tamari
1 clove garlic

Add all ingredients to a high-speed blender and blend until completely combined.

Vegan Ranch Dressing

*How do you take a healthy garden salad and make it instantly un-healthy? Ranch dressing tastes so good but also packs in **a lot** of fat! Here, we have the same great taste and creamy texture without the oil—so pour on!*

MAKES 1¼ CUPS

1 cup Eggless Mayo (see **Odds and Ends**)
3 Tbsp water
2 tsp fresh parsley, finely minced
½ tsp ground black pepper
¼ tsp garlic powder
¼ tsp onion powder
3 drops liquid smoke

Add all ingredients to a small mixing bowl, and whisk together. Pour into a dressing bottle and serve.

Note: This is a close cousin of tzatziki sauce; they share similar ingredients. If you want to do some quick magic, peel and dice a Persian cucumber and mix with the dressing, and you have tzatziki sauce!

Za'atar Dressing

Let this blend of herbs and spices dress up your garden salad with a Middle-Eastern flair!

MAKES 1¾ CUPS

1 cup water
⅔ cup raw cashews
Juice of ½ lemon
1 Tbsp apple cider vinegar
3 tsp chopped fresh thyme leaves (or 1 tsp dried thyme)
2 tsp sumac
2 tsp white sesame seeds
2 tsp nigella seeds
½ tsp sea salt
¼ tsp ground black pepper

Blend the water and cashews, then add remaining ingredients into a dressing bottle and shake well.

Note: The reason to blend only the cashews and water together, then separately mixing in the remaining ingredients, is that if you add all the ingredients to a blender at one, it will come out gray—not exactly the most appetizing color for a salad dressing! That's the same for the other salad dressings in this chapter that include fresh herbs, which turn the dressing green when blended.

Carrot Ginger Dressing

Similar to what is commonly found in Japanese restaurants, this dressing is a healthier sweet-and-sour addition to salads!

MAKES 2½ CUPS

½ cup raw cashews
1 cup water
⅓ cup apple cider vinegar
1 Tbsp tamari
1 Tbsp toasted sesame oil
2 medium carrots, chopped into 1" segments
2" fresh ginger
1 medium shallot
1 clove garlic
3 Medjool dates

Blend the cashews, water, apple cider vinegar, tamari, and sesame oil first until smooth, then add remaining ingredients and blend for several minutes to puree the carrots thoroughly.

Chipotle Southwest Dressing

This creamy, smoky dressing has just the right kick to spice up a garden salad!

MAKES 1½ CUPS

1 cup Eggless Mayo (see **Odds and Ends**)
1 Tbsp + 1 tsp lime juice
2 Medjool dates
1 tsp smoked paprika
1 tsp apple cider vinegar
½ tsp sea salt
½ tsp garlic powder
½ tsp chipotle powder
Pinch of dried thyme and ground cumin
2 tsp fresh cilantro, chopped
1 tsp water

Combine all ingredients in a high-speed blender except for the cilantro and water, and blend until smooth. Pour into a dressing bottle, add the chopped cilantro, and shake well. Add water to thin as needed, and serve.

Raspberry Vinaigrette

Fruit vinaigrettes add a unique flavor to salads, but they typically include a lot of oil and sugar. Here, we use fresh whole-food ingredients for a healthier version that's big on taste and friendlier for your heart!

MAKES 2 CUPS

½ cup raw cashews
1 cup water
½ cup raspberries (frozen is fine, but thaw first)
1 Medjool date
¼ cup balsamic vinegar
¼ tsp white miso

Combine all ingredients in a high-speed blender, then add to a dressing bottle and serve.

Mango Mustard Dressing

The combination of sweet mango and tangy mustard make a delicious dressing that's bright and beautiful!

MAKES 1¼ CUPS

1 cup frozen mango chunks, thawed
¼ cup tahini
¼ cup apple cider vinegar
2 Tbsp yellow mustard
2 Medjool dates
1 tsp sea salt

Blend all ingredients in a high-speed blender, and serve.

Thousand Island Dressing

Thousand Island Dressing is normally full of mayonnaise and oil, but in this slimmed-down version you won't miss all the fat, and at the same time you'll enjoy the familiar combination of sweet relish, tomato, and savory garlic and onion!

MAKES ¾ CUP

½ cup Eggless Mayo (see **Odds and Ends**)
2 Tbsp French Dressing (see **Salads and Dressings**), or ketchup
½ medium shallot, minced
3 tsp sweet pickle relish
1 tsp apple cider vinegar
1 tsp agave nectar
¼ tsp garlic powder
¼ tsp sea salt

Combine all ingredients and mix well before using.

Super Soups

I have to be honest: when I go out to eat, soups are not high on my list of things to try. I'm just not *souper* into it. I'm not going to waste your time with soups like minestrone, which is pretty much just soggy pasta and overcooked vegetables. If I'm going to have soup, I want it to be *souper* good.

Super Soups as a System

It's hard to beat soup for convenience: Once you throw the ingredients together in a big pot, just walk away and an hour later you have many meals worth of lunch and dinner. This is where I break out my Mason jars for freezing, either pint jars for single servings or quarts for family size. Make sure you don't fill the jar past the freezer line. This way, you can grab lunch on the way out the door that is *souper* good and *souper* convenient.

Super Soups

Fragrant Coconut Thai Soup

It's not difficult to turn this traditional Thai soup into a whole-food, healthy treat. The combination of lime, ginger, and lemongrass make this soup wonderfully fragrant and irresistible.

MAKES 7 CUPS

2 cloves garlic
2 medium shallots
½ cup coconut butter/manna
2" thumb of galangal, or ginger
1 Tbsp minced lemongrass
3 Medjool dates
4 cups water
Juice of 2 limes
Large handful of shiitake mushrooms, sliced into ¼" wide strips
3 scallions, diced
2 Tbsp tamari
One 16 oz. block extra-firm tofu, cut into 1" cubes
1 tsp sea salt
1 Tbsp sriracha
1 cup mung bean sprouts
½ cup fresh cilantro, chopped
1 cup cherry tomatoes, halved

Add the ingredients listed from garlic to water to a high-speed blender, and blend until smooth. Pour into a large saucepan and add the ingredients listed from lime juice to sriracha, and cook on medium heat for 10 minutes, covered. Add the mung bean sprouts, cilantro, and cherry tomatoes, and continue to cook for another 5 minutes before serving.

Broccoli Cheezy Soup

Smokey and tangy, this soup is perfectly hearty for when the temperatures outside are dropping.

MAKES 10 CUPS

½ cup raw cashews
5½ cups water
¾ cup all-purpose flour
⅔ cup nutritional yeast
1 medium yellow onion, roughly chopped
1 yellow bell pepper, seeded and roughly chopped
1 Tbsp ground mustard
1 tsp turmeric powder
1 Tbsp Better Than Bouillon, Vegetable flavor
2 tsp sea salt
1 tsp smoked paprika
3 cups fresh, or frozen (thawed), broccoli
1½ cups Bacony Vegan Bits (see **Odds and Ends**)

Add the cashews and water to a high-speed blender, and blend until smooth. Add the flour, nutritional yeast, onion, bell pepper, ground mustard, and turmeric, and blend for another two minutes, then pour into a large saucepan. Add the bouillon, salt, and paprika, and cook on medium heat for 10 minutes, stirring regularly.

While the soup is cooking, add the broccoli to a food processor and pulse until the broccoli is chopped well, then add to the soup. Continue to stir and cook the soup for several more minutes, then stir in the Bacony Vegan Bits and serve.

Lebanese Red Lentil Soup

This soup is a staple in my kitchen because it's easy to prepare, it's packed full of whole-food, unprocessed ingredients, and tastes so good!

MAKES 8½ CUPS

6 cups water
⅓ cup raw cashews
1 medium yellow onion
1 clove garlic
1 small carrot
2 green olives
2 cups red lentils (rinsed and strained)
1 Tbsp chopped fresh parsley
1 Tbsp chopped fresh mint
2 Tbsp Better Than Bouillon, Vegetable flavor
1 tsp ground cumin
1 tsp turmeric powder
1 tsp sea salt
¼ tsp ground black pepper
Juice of 1 lemon

Add the water, cashews, onion, garlic, carrot, and olives to a high-speed blender, and blend for several minutes until completely smooth.

Transfer to a large saucepan and add remaining ingredients except for the lemon juice, and bring to a boil. Partially cover and cook over medium-low heat for 30 minutes, stirring every 5 minutes. Once the lentils are soft, add the lemon juice, and serve. If you wish for the soup to be completely smooth, use an immersion blender to puree before serving.

Roasted Roots Soup

Roasting the vegetables may be an additional step, but it gives this soup an added depth of flavor that's well worth the effort!

MAKES 8 CUPS

6 large carrots
2 large parsnips
1 medium red onion
1 thumb-sized piece of ginger
4 cloves garlic, unpeeled
6 cups water
½ cup raw cashews
2 Tbsp Better Than Bouillon, No Chicken flavor

Preheat the oven to 450° F. Slice the carrots and parsnips length-wise, then cut into 4" sections and add to a lined baking sheet. Cut the onion in half and put each half cut-side down on the baking sheet. Slice the thumb of ginger in half, and add each half to the cooking sheet. Use a high-temperature cooking spray to coat the vegetables, and bake for 15 minutes. Turn the carrots, parsnips, and ginger over and spray again. Wrap the unpeeled garlic cloves in aluminum foil and place on the baking sheet, and return to the oven for another 20 minutes.

In a high-speed blender, add 2 cups of the water with the cashews and blend until smooth. Add the carrots, parsnips, on-ion, ginger, and squeeze the garlic cloves out of the peels, and blend until smooth. Pour the blended ingredients into a large saucepan and stir in the remaining 4 cups of water and the bouil-lon. Cook and stir the soup on medium heat until hot enough to serve.

Zuppa Toscana

With spicy Italian-seasoned vegan sausage, potatoes, and kale, this soup is the definition of hearty and heart-healthy.

MAKES 10 CUPS

5 cloves garlic, crushed
½ cup raw cashews
6 cups water
3 large Yukon gold potatoes, cubed in ½" pieces
3 leeks, chopped and rinsed well
2 cups chopped kale
1 cup cubed Italian-Style Vegan Sausage (see **Odds and Ends**)
½ cup nutritional yeast
2 bay leaves
2 Tbsp Better Than Bouillon, Vegetable flavor
1 tsp sea salt
1 tsp ground black pepper
½ tsp chipotle powder
¼ cup Bacony Vegan Bits (see **Odds and Ends**)

Blend the garlic, cashews, and water in a high-speed blender until smooth, then pour into a large saucepan. I recommend using a food processor to chop the kale into small pieces, and use an air fryer or frying pan to cook the vegan sausage pieces for 5 minutes before adding to the soup. Add the remaining ingredients and cook on medium heat for 20 minutes, then remove the bay leaves and serve the soup topped with Bacony Vegan Bits.

Creamy Tomato Soup

After tasting this fresh tomato soup, someone in my Fresh Whole-Food Soups class remarked that it "actually tastes like what's in it": fresh tomatoes! A welcome change from tomato soup from the can, once you try this Creamy Tomato Soup, you'll be sold too.

MAKES 5 CUPS

7 medium tomatoes
1 medium yellow onion, diced
1 medium carrot, diced
4 cloves garlic, diced
½ cup raw cashews
1 cup water
1 tsp sea salt
½ tsp ground black pepper
2 Medjool dates
5 sprigs of fresh thyme
Pinch of baking soda

In a high-speed blender, puree five of the tomatoes and pour into a large saucepan. Add the two tomatoes with the remaining ingredients except for the thyme and baking soda into the blender and blend until smooth, then add to the saucepan. Add the sprigs of thyme, set to medium heat, and cover until the soup is bubbling. Then reduce the heat to medium-low and keep covered, stirring occasionally. Cook for 30 minutes, remove the thyme sprigs, and add the baking soda. Stir for another minute and serve.

Split Pea Soup

This recipe has everything I like: creamy split peas and a smoky salty flavor without the ham. Let the pigs be pigs, and enjoy this nourishing, hearty soup!

MAKES 9 CUPS

2¼ cups dried yellow split peas
1 medium white onion, chopped
5 cloves garlic, crushed
3 celery stalks, diced
6 cups water
2 tsp sea salt
1 tsp turmeric powder
1 tsp Better Than Bouillon, Vegetable flavor
1 tsp liquid smoke
½ tsp ground black pepper

This recipe works best in a slow cooker, otherwise you might end up with some uncooked split peas. Add all the ingredients to a slow cooker and cook on high for 6 hours.

Mighty Miso Soup

Combining the nutrient powers of dashi (mushroom broth) with sea-weed and miso paste, this whole-food soup is a fresh take on a traditional Japanese recipe.

MAKES 3 CUPS

2½ cups water
1 dried shiitake mushroom cap
1 tsp dried wakame seaweed
½ box 12.5 oz. Mori-Nu silken tofu, cut into ½" cubes
2 Tbsp mellow white miso paste
2 scallions, chopped

Bring the water to a boil in a medium saucepan. Shut off the heat, add the mushroom cap and wakame, and soak for 15 minutes.

Use a fork to remove the wakame and set aside, then transfer the mushroom and water to a blender and blend for 1 minute. Return to saucepan and add the wakame back in. Add the tofu cubes and simmer for 2 minutes. Turn off the heat, and remove about ½ cup of the broth into a small bowl and mix the miso paste with the broth, then return to the saucepan, add the scallions, and mix well.

"No Beef, No Bull" Stew

Beef soup in a can may be a health nightmare, but this heart-healthy version will warm your tummy and let you sleep easy.

MAKES 9½ CUPS

6 cups water
4 whole carrots, peeled and cut into rounds (save the peels)
2 medium tomatoes
1 medium onion
3 cloves garlic
1 Tbsp Better Than Bouillon, No Beef flavor
1 bag of Butler Soy Curls, or 2 cups Vegan Ground "Meat" Crumbles (see **Odds and Ends**)
2 cups red potatoes, unpeeled and cut into ½" pieces
1 cup button mushrooms, finely chopped
2 bay leaves
1 Tbsp blackstrap molasses
1 tsp dried thyme
1 tsp sea salt
1 tsp ground black pepper
2 Tbsp cornstarch

Add 4 cups of the water, carrot peels, tomatoes, onion, and garlic to a blender, and blend until smooth. Pour into a large saucepan and bring to a boil, then add the bouillon and soy curls, cover the saucepan, and let sit for 30 minutes.

Add the remaining 2 cups of water and the remaining ingredients except for the cornstarch, stir well, and bring to a simmer and cover for 30 minutes.

Drain 1 cup of the liquid from the stew and whisk in the cornstarch, then stir the cornstarch slurry back into the saucepan. Continue to simmer uncovered for 15 minutes and stir several times. Remove the bay leaves and serve.

Note: Butler Soy Curls is a meat alternative that comes dried and is made from whole soybeans. They are sold at natural food stores and online. If you prefer to use the Vegan Ground "Meat" Crumbles, follow that recipe but instead of using a food processor to make crumbles, chop the sausages whole, and either air-fry or panfry for 5 minutes before adding to the soup. If you use the crumbles recipe instead of the Butler Soy Curls, eliminate 1 cup of water from the soup recipe, and you can skip the 30-minute soaking time in the instructions above.

Unconventional Black Bean Soup

This black bean soup has a lot of parents: Cuban, Mexican, and Scottish (that's me). When it comes to food, I don't draw boundaries, I'm happy to take different aspects of traditional recipes and mix them together to see what happens. Ethnically, I'm a mutt, a combination of many different European countries, so I'm not shy about trying the same thing with food!

MAKES 7 CUPS

2 cups water
2 carrots, roughly chopped
3 ribs celery, roughly chopped
3 cups cooked black beans
1 medium yellow onion, chopped
½ cup Sofrito (see **Odd and Ends**)
½ tsp liquid smoke
2 tsp ground cumin
2 tsp dried oregano
1 jalapeno pepper, seeded and diced
1 tsp sea salt
Juice of ½ lime
Handful of chopped fresh cilantro

Add the water, carrots, celery, and 1 cup of cooked black beans to a blender and blend until completely pureed. Pour into a large saucepan and add the remaining ingredients from the 2 cups of black beans to the salt. Bring the soup to a simmer, then add the lime juice, and serve with chopped cilantro sprinkled on top of the soup. You can also serve the soup over ½ cup of brown rice if you'd like.

Smoky Bourbon Chili

When I set out to write a vegan chili recipe, I wanted to make something unique and delicious, so I combined hearty, whole-food ingredients with a rich hint of bourbon and smoky fire.

MAKES 5 CUPS

1 large red onion, sliced lengthwise
3 cloves garlic, minced
6 large tomatoes
6 Medjool dates
1½ cups cooked kidney beans
1½ Tbsp ground cumin
1½ tsp ground coriander
1 tsp smoked paprika
1 tsp chipotle powder
2 tsp sea salt
¼ tsp ground black pepper
1 Tbsp Better Than Bouillon, No Beef flavor
One 8 oz. package of tempeh
¼ cup bourbon
1 Tbsp tamari
1 tsp liquid smoke

In a large saucepan, water-sauté the onion and garlic for several minutes. Add two of the tomatoes and all the dates to a high-speed blender and puree. Chop the remaining four tomatoes, and add these and the puree to the saucepan. Stir in the remaining ingredients through the bouillon, cover, and simmer for 30 minutes.

While the chili is simmering, preheat the oven to 350° F. Cube the tempeh and add to a food processor with an "S" blade, and process until the tempeh is crumbled. Spread the crumbles out on a baking sheet, and bake for 10 minutes. Remove and stir well, then bake for an additional 10 minutes. Add the tempeh to a mixing bowl with the bourbon, tamari, and liquid smoke, and stir until well combined. Spread the mixture back onto the baking sheet and place it back into the oven (now turned off), and keep it in the warm oven to dry the mixture while the chili is cooking.

Once the chili has simmered for 30 minutes, shut off the heat and stir in the tempeh mixture, and serve.

Corn Chowder House Rules

I'll stack up my creamy corn chowder against anyone's non-vegan recipe—creamy, nourishing, and bursting with flavor, this chowder rules!

MAKES 11½ CUPS

5 cups water
⅔ cup raw cashews
⅓ cup coconut manna
3 cups frozen corn
1 red bell pepper, chopped, or ½ cup chopped roasted red pepper
2 celery stalks, diced
1 medium yellow onion, chopped
2 medium Yukon gold potatoes, scrubbed well, unpeeled, cut into ½" cubes
1 bay leaf
2 tsp sea salt
1 tsp dried thyme
½ tsp ground black pepper
1 tsp natural butter flavoring
½ cup Bacony Vegan Bits (see **Odds and Ends**)

In a high-speed blender, combine the water, cashews, coconut manna, and 1 cup of the corn, and blend for several minutes until completely smooth.

In a large saucepan, water-sauté the bell pepper, celery, and onion for several minutes. Add the liquid from the blender and the remaining ingredients except for the Bacony Vegan Bits, cover, and simmer for 20 minutes (until potatoes are fork-tender). Stir in the bacon bits, remove the bay leaf, and serve.

Sambar (Indian Lentil Soup)

Curry leaves and spices drive this vegetable soup in a delightfully different direction: to India!

MAKES 7 CUPS

1 cup toor dal (yellow split pigeon peas)
2½ cups water
1 tsp sea salt
½ tsp turmeric powder
3 cloves garlic, crushed
1 medium yellow onion,
8 curry leaves
1½ cups water
⅓ cup raw cashews
Juice of ½ lemon
1 Tbsp tamarind paste
1½ cups chopped fresh vegetables (eggplant, carrot, zucchini)
1 medium tomato, chopped
1 Tbsp Sambar Powder (see **Odds and Ends**)
1 tsp chili powder
1 tsp salt
Fresh cilantro (to garnish)

The quickest way to cook the toor dal is to use a pressure cooker; I set my Instant Pot for 10 minutes on the manual setting and add the Toor Dal, 2½ cups water, sea salt, and turmeric. When finished cooking, use an immersion blender to puree the lentils.

In a large saucepan, add the garlic, onion, and curry leaves, and water-sauté until the onions are soft, stirring often. Blend the water, cashews, lemon juice, and tamarind paste in a high-powered blender until smooth, then add to the saucepan with the chopped vegetables, tomato, and Sambar Powder. Stir and cover, and simmer for 10–15 minutes, until the vegetables are fork-tender. Garnish with chopped fresh cilantro.

Note: For the sake of convenience and using what's on hand, sometimes I use frozen mixed vegetables from the supermarket. Not exactly the most authentic, I know, but Sambar is supposed to be a spicy lentil soup with mixed vegetables, so feel free to use whatever mixed veggies you want, and don't worry about the food police.

African Peanut Soup

Smooth and creamy, sweet and spicy, this soup is a blend of great tastes.

MAKES 8 CUPS

3 cups water
1 Tbsp Berbere Spice Mix (see **Odds and Ends**)
1 cup creamy peanut butter
1 tsp sea salt
1 ripe plantain, almost black in color (or substitute a just-yellow
    banana if needed)
1 medium yellow onion
1 orange or yellow bell pepper
3 large cloves garlic
2 medium tomatoes
½ cup coconut manna
1 large sweet potato
1" thumb of ginger
1 Tbsp Better Than Bouillon, No Chicken flavor
Fresh cilantro, chopped (for garnish)
Roasted peanuts (for garish)

Add the soup ingredients to a high-powered blender and blend until smooth.

Pour into a large saucepan and bring to a simmer on medium heat, then cover and cook for 25 minutes.

Serve topped with chopped cilantro and chopped roasted peanuts.

Naked Burrito Stew

*I have probably eaten my weight in Trader Joe's vegetarian burritos. There was a bleak period of life where for several years they stopped carrying them, and I wonder if my protesting in front of the store every weekend made them change their mind and bring them back. Anyway, I unintentionally stumbled my way into making a stew that tasted similar, and I realized after looking at the ingredients label that my stew had many of the same ingredients as the aforementioned burrito. So I tweaked the recipe further and got it to taste **very** similar. Enjoy this stew as it is, or add cornstarch to thicken it and then use it as a filling for burritos!*

MAKES 8½ CUPS

1 cup water
1 medium onion, chopped
3 cloves garlic, minced
1½ cups Yukon gold potatoes, peeled and cut into ½" cubes
1 green bell pepper, diced
2 medium tomatoes, chopped
1 cup cooked black beans
1 cup cooked pinto beans
2 cups frozen corn, thawed
1 Anaheim green chili, seeded and diced
1 Tbsp Better Than Bouillon, Vegetable flavor
2 tsp ground cumin
2 tsp smoked paprika
1 tsp sea salt
1 tsp dried oregano
¼ cup fresh cilantro, chopped

In a blender, combine the water, onion, and garlic, and blend until completely smooth.

Add the mixture to a large saucepan, and add the remaining ingredients except for the cilantro. Bring to a simmer and cover, cooking for 20 minutes or until the potatoes are tender. Stir in the cilantro, and serve.

Ful Mudammas

There are different ways to make this Middle Eastern dish depending on the region—breakfast, appetizer, stew. . . . I'm going to call this a bean stew and put it in the Soups chapter so it has somewhere to live in this cookbook. Whatever you want to call it, grab some fresh pita bread at the supermarket and tear off pieces to use to scoop up this delicious dish!

MAKES 3 CUPS

1½ cups cooked split yellow fava beans
⅔ cup cooked chickpeas
1 small red onion, chopped into strips
5 cloves of garlic, crushed
3 Roma tomatoes
Juice of 1 lemon
2 green olives, pitted and minced
¾ tsp ground cumin
¼ tsp ground coriander
1 tsp sea salt
¼ cup chopped fresh parsley

Soak the dried fava beans and chickpeas together overnight, then cook them together on the stovetop or in a pressure cooker. You don't need to be exact in measuring the beans, but I prefer a ⅓:⅔ ratio of chickpeas to fava beans.

In a large saucepan, water-sauté the onion and garlic for several minutes, then add the beans. Use a masher to very roughly mash the beans so that the beans are just broken up but not enough to turn them into paste. Add the tomatoes, lemon juice, olives, cumin, coriander, and salt, and mix. Stir frequently over medium heat for about 10 minutes, stirring in water as needed to keep the mixture from sticking and to keep it as a stew. Add the parsley and cover, cook for an additional minute, and then serve with triangles of fresh pita strips.

Note: I've had large fava beans from a can, frozen, or cooked from dry beans, but I find them to be too sour and the skins are tough. Split yellow fava beans is my personal preference, and you can find them at Mediterranean markets or order them online; they have great flavor and texture that isn't sour like the larger variety.

Mushroom Madeira Risotto

The rich, buttery taste of Madeira wine lends a unique flavor to this mushroom risotto, a sweet and savory delight!

MAKES 7 CUPS

½ cup raw cashews
½ cup hot water + ½ cup fresh water
1 shallot, minced
2 cups mushrooms of your choice, roughly chopped
1 cup uncooked arborio rice
3 cups water
1 Tbsp Better Than Bouillon, Mushroom flavor
1 Tbsp nutritional yeast
Juice of ½ lemon
2 cups fresh spinach, stems removed
⅓ cup Madeira wine
1 tsp dried rosemary
1 tsp sea salt
½ tsp ground black pepper
½ tsp dried thyme
¼ tsp onion powder

Soak the cashews in the hot water for 15 minutes to soften. Drain the soaking water and add to a high-speed blender with ½ cup of fresh water, and blend until smooth, then set aside.

Water-sauté the shallot and mushrooms in a large cast-iron frying pan until soft, then add the rice, water, and bouillon. Bring to a boil then cover, cook for 10 minutes on low heat, then stir, cover, and continue to cook for another 5 minutes.

Add the cashew mixture and the remaining ingredients, and cook uncovered for an additional 5 minutes. Make sure that the rice is tender, and serve.

Autumn White Bean Soup

As the temperature outside drops, I like to turn to heartier veggies of the fall harvest for a warm and filling soup that will light up my taste buds.

MAKES 14 CUPS

6 cups water
½ cup raw cashews
1 medium yellow onion, roughly chopped
4 cloves garlic
1" fresh ginger
1 medium carrot, diced
1 stalk celery, diced
1 orange or yellow bell pepper, seeded and chopped
1 medium butternut squash, peeled and cubed (approximately 4
      cups chopped)
2 medium sweet potatoes, peeled and cubed (approximately 2–3
      cups chopped)
1½ cups cooked white beans such as great northern or cannellini
1 Tbsp Better Than Bouillon, Mushroom flavor
1 tsp turmeric powder
1 tsp ground cinnamon
1 tsp sage
2 tsp sea salt
¼ tsp ground nutmeg
1 bay leaf

In a high-speed blender, combine the water, cashews, onion, garlic, and ginger, and blend until smooth.

Add to a large saucepan and add the carrots, celery, bell pepper, butternut squash, and sweet potatoes, and cook for 20 minutes until the potatoes and squash are easily pierced with a fork. Add the remaining ingredients and continue to cook for an additional 10 minutes, then serve.

Meals

Burgers and Balls

That's right, this section is called Burgers and Balls. And I'm not talking about a cookout at a nudist colony. I'm putting these two together because, really, aren't veggie burgers and veggie balls pretty much the same thing but in different shapes?

This chapter is full of veggie burgers made from different grains and beans with veggies, herbs, and spices mixed in. It's more of a whole-food approach to making veggie burgers than trying to replicate the taste of a hamburger; I like to think of these recipes as their own thing, standing on their own instead of trying to be something else. Even the recipes that have familiar names, like the Vegan Corned Beef Hash Burger or the Swedish-Style Vegan Meatballs, use spices and herbs similar to their meat versions, but I'm not trying to fool anyone with it. Think of them like cousins instead of twins.

These recipes can cross over into some of the other chapters here: combine the Falafel with the Lemon Tahini Sauce and Pickled Turnips, and you have a stellar falafel wrap for lunch. How about adding some Nacho Cheese Sauce to the Black Bean Burger with some sliced tomato and avocado? The Italian-Style Vegan Meatballs go perfectly with the Sundried Tomato Marinara Sauce over pasta, sprinkled with Parmesan-Like Topping.

This is a good opportunity to use an air fryer if you have one in order to make these recipes oil free. You can always use some spray oil to lightly coat the veggie burger and veggie balls and bake them in the oven if you don't have an air fryer, or use a little oil and fry them on a cast-iron frying pan—just make sure to use a good metal spatula. Of all three methods, the air fryer works the best, especially for the veggie balls because it makes the outside crispy. Sometimes using a little spray oil before using the air fryer gives them a little extra crisp.

One important rule to follow when making veggie burgers and veggie balls is to use cooked grains, beans, and veggies before mixing the ingredients together. The outside of these veggie burgers and balls will get crispy while the insides are soft, and if the ingredients aren't already cooked, the insides will taste raw and too strong or unpleasant. But, hey, one bonus of eating veggie burgers and veggie balls instead of meat is that you don't need to worry about your food killing you if it's not cooked long enough.

Burgers and Balls as a System

I like to make these recipes in batches and store them in the freezer to use when I want them. I stack the burgers together in sealable plastic freezer bags, and I throw the balls all together into a sealable freezer bag.

This chapter uses many of the same ingredients as the other chapters but in a different form as a delivery system for eating healthy foods: many of these recipes are similar to what you'd find in a bowl meal—beans, grains, veggies—but are processed and cooked to be eaten as a burger instead. You can eat these veggie burgers with burger buns, burger thins, bread, in a wrap, or between leaves of lettuce; it's up to you!

Burgers and Balls

My Favorite Falafel Recipe

I love the taste of falafel, but I've been looking for a healthier alter-native to deep-frying; that's why I got an air fryer in the first place! This recipe combines delicious flavors I love—parsley, cilantro, fava beans, onion, garlic, and spices—to make a fresh and healthy falafel sandwich that I could eat every day.

MAKES 18 BALLS

1½ cups cooked chickpeas
1 bunch flat-leaf parsley
1½ cups cooked small yellow split fava beans
1 bunch fresh cilantro
1 medium yellow onion
6 cloves garlic, crushed
2 Tbsp chickpea flour
3 tsp ground cumin
1 tsp ground coriander
1 tsp baking soda
1 tsp sea salt

Add the chickpeas and parsley to a food processor, and process until well combined. Empty mixture into a large mixing bowl, then add the remaining ingredients to the food processor, and process them until well combined. Add to the mixing bowl.

Mix the ingredients together and roll balls of the mixture and flatten somewhat to form small 2" wide patties. Spray the falafels with cooking spray and bake in an air fryer for 10 minutes at 370° F. Then use a spatula to flip, then spray and cook for an additional 8 minutes. (Alternatively, you can bake in an oven for 10 minutes at 370° F, spray and flip, then bake for an additional 8 minutes; or panfry them.)

Note: You can cook the falafel without any oil if that is your preference, but it does affect the texture; it's not as crispy on the outside. You can also make falafel burger patties with this recipe.

Recommended with: Fresh pita bread, Lemon Tahini Sauce (see **Bowls and Sauces**), chopped romaine lettuce, Pickled Turnip (see **Odds and Ends**), chopped fresh tomato.

Samosa Patties

I love Samosas at Indian Restaurants, but they are usually deep-fried, so they're not something I have often. These Samosa Patties have the same delicious taste but without all the oil!

MAKES 4 PATTIES

2 medium Russet potatoes, peeled and cubed
½ cup frozen peas, thawed
2 medium shallots, minced
Juice of ½ lemon
¼ cup fresh cilantro, chopped
2 tsp fresh grated ginger
1 tsp ground cumin
½ tsp sea salt
½ tsp garlic powder
¼ tsp turmeric powder
½ cup chickpea flour
½ tsp fine black salt

Boil the potatoes until fork-tender, then drain and cool. In a large metal mixing bowl, mash the potatoes then add the remaining ingredients except for the chickpea flour and black salt. Stir the mixture until well combined, then form four patties from the mixture.

Combine the chickpea flour with the black salt, then coat the patties in the mixture, and panfry for several minutes on each side until golden brown.

Recommended with: In a small bowl, combine ½ cup Eggless Mayo (see **Odds and Ends**) with 2 Tbsp tamarind sauce and use this as a sauce for the Samosa Patties.

Indian Masala Burgers

These delicious burgers are full of whole-food, healthy ingredients with a delightful twist of curry.

MAKES 6 PATTIES

2 large Yukon Gold potatoes, peeled and cubed
½ cup chopped carrots
½ cup oat flour
½ cup cooked chickpeas
½ cup chopped yellow onions
½ cup frozen corn kernels
½ cup green bell pepper, chopped
⅓ cup fresh cilantro, chopped
2 cloves garlic, grated
1" thumb fresh ginger, grated
1 Tbsp Blasphemous Curry Powder (see **Odds and Ends**)
½ tsp sea salt
¼ tsp mustard seed
½ cup chickpea flour

Using a non-stick pan, water-sauté the potato cubes and carrots until tender, then add the remaining ingredients except the chickpea flour and continue to cook until all vegetables are cooked.

Add the mixture to a food processor and pulse until they are well combined; the idea is to blend them just enough for everything to be chopped but not so much that it becomes a paste.

Form the mixture into six patties, and coat the top and bottom of each patty with chickpea flour before panfrying.

Note: You can use a spice grinder, food processor, or blender to process rolled oats into oat flour if you don't have prepared oat flour already.

Recommended with: Slices of fresh tomato, Eggless Mayo (see **Odds and Ends**) mixed with Blasphemous Curry Powder (see **Odds and Ends**) to make a condiment sauce.

Gobi Manchurian Patties

Gobi Manchurian is a delicious Indo-Chinese blend of tangy and sweet tomato glaze covering fried cauliflower, and in this recipe I've re-created the same combination of flavors in a patty with a whole-food spin.

MAKES 8 PATTIES

FOR THE PATTIES:
½ head cauliflower, with florets removed from stem
⅓ cup chopped scallions
½ green bell pepper, chopped
1 stalk celery, chopped
2 cloves garlic, minced
2 tsp sea salt
1½ cups cooked chickpeas
½ cup potato flakes
½" thumb fresh ginger, minced

FOR THE SAUCE:
One 6 oz. can tomato paste
3 Tbsp apple cider vinegar
2 Tbsp agave nectar
1 Tbsp tamari
1½ tsp sea salt
1 tsp sriracha
¼ tsp ground black pepper
½ cup water
1 tsp cornstarch

Boil the cauliflower florets until tender, strain, and set aside. Water-sauté the scallions, bell pepper, celery, garlic, and salt.

Combine with the remaining patty ingredients in a large metal mixing bowl and mash until well combined, or add patty ingredients to a food processor and pulse until well combined. Form the mixture into patties and panfry for 5 minutes on each side.

To make the sauce, combine all ingredients in a small saucepan except the water in cornstarch. In a bowl, combine the water and cornstarch to form a slurry, then add the saucepan. Cook the sauce on medium heat for 5 minutes and stir frequently until the sauce has thickened.

Once the patties have cooked, coat with the sauce and serve.

Sushi Rice Patties

This recipe combines all my favorite flavors for vegan nori rolls but without the extra step of rolling and cutting; my boys are big fans of nori rolls and couldn't believe how good these Sushi Rice Patties tasted when they first tried them!

MAKES 6 PATTIES

1 sheet nori, torn into pieces
1 cup cooked chickpeas
½ cup panko bread crumbs
1 medium carrot, chopped and cooked until tender
1 Haas avocado
1 Tbsp apple cider vinegar
1 Tbsp agave nectar
1 Tbsp tamari
1 tsp sea salt
1 cup panko bread crumbs
2 Tbsp unhulled sesame seeds
2 cups cooked short-grain brown rice (cooked with 1" piece of kombu seaweed, optional)

Add the nori and chickpeas to a food processor and run until the pieces have been broken down into flakes. Add the remaining ingredients to the food processor, including the kombu from the rice (if using), and pulse until well combined.

Form the mixture into patties and press them on a plate of breadcrumbs on each side, then panfry the patties for 5 minutes on each side.

Recommended with: You can serve the patties open with pickled ginger and wasabi paste, or as veggie burger patties with A Different Kind of Dashi Sauce (see **Bowls and Sauces**).

Cuban Black Bean Burgers

This recipe is a delicious trip to Cuba, showcasing just how great a combination of whole-food ingredients with Cuban spices can taste.

MAKES 6 PATTIES

¼ cup red onion, chopped
2 cloves garlic, crushed
½ green bell pepper
2 cups cooked black beans
1 cup cooked short-grain brown rice (cooked with 1 bay leaf, optional)
½ cup quick oats
1 Tbsp lime juice
1 tsp ground cumin
1 tsp smoked paprika
1 tsp sea salt
½ tsp liquid smoke
½ cup cornmeal

Water-sauté the onion, garlic, and green pepper until they are soft. Reserve ⅔ cup of the black beans, and add the rice, beans, and remaining ingredients to a food processor and pulse until ingredients are well combined. Add the reserved black beans and mix well, and let the burger mixture set for 20 minutes before forming patties.

Coat the patties in the cornmeal and panfry for 5 minutes on each side, then serve.

Recommended with: Sliced avocado, Eggless Mayo (see **Odds and Ends**) mixed with a small spoonful of sriracha.

Sweet Jamaican Veggie Burgers

I love the spices of Jamaica—nutmeg, allspice, cumin, paprika—but it can be hard to find vegetarian options with these flavors where I live, so I decided to create my own veggie burger that combines these delicious flavors so I can enjoy them whenever I want.

MAKES 5 PATTIES

¼ cup red onion, chopped
2 cloves garlic, crushed
2 cups cooked kidney beans
1½ cup cooked sweet potatoes
½ cup frozen peas, thawed
½ cup frozen corn, thawed
¼ cup oat flour
1 Tbsp blackstrap molasses
1 tsp ground cumin
1 tsp smoked paprika
1 tsp sea salt
½ tsp ground allspice
½ tsp chipotle powder
¼ tsp ground cinnamon
¼ tsp ground nutmeg

Water-sauté the onions and garlic until soft, then add to a food processor with the rest of the ingredients and pulse until well combined.

Let stand for 15 minutes, then form into patties and panfry 5 minutes on each side until browned.

Recommended with: Slices of avocado and Jamaican Jerk Sauce (see **Bowls and Sauces**).

Ethiopian Veggie Burgers

If you've ever been to an Ethiopian restaurant, you know how unique and amazing the dishes can be. In this recipe, I combine some of my favorite Ethiopian flavors in an untraditional way.

MAKES 8 PATTIES

1 cup cooked teff (from ⅓ cup uncooked teff)
1 cup cooked sweet potato
1 ½ cups cooked kidney beans
½ cup quick oats
½ cup frozen spinach, thawed and pressed
3 cloves garlic
1" fresh ginger
2 Tbsp Berbere Spice Mix (see **Odds and Ends**)
1 tsp turmeric powder
1 tsp sea salt

Combine all ingredients in a food processor and pulse until the mixture is well blended. Let the mixture set for 20 minutes, then form into patties and panfry 5 minutes on each side.

Recommended with: Slices of fresh tomato and Eggless Mayo (see **Odds and Ends**) mixed with Berbere Spice Mix (see **Odds and Ends**) to make a sauce for the burgers.

Afghani Spinach Burger

Looking for new ways to add some more dark leafy greens onto your plate? This Afghani Spinach Burger is loaded with the power of greens, and it's a lot more fun to eat than a side of cooked spinach!

MAKES 6 PATTIES

½ green bell pepper, finely chopped
1½ cups cooked kidney beans
1½ cups cooked short-grain brown rice
1 cup frozen spinach, thawed and pressed
2 tsp ground coriander
1 tsp garlic powder
½ tsp ground cumin
½ tsp onion powder
1 tsp sea salt
½ tsp ground black pepper

Sauté the bell pepper until soft, the add to a food processor with the remaining ingredients and pulse until well combined. Form into patties and panfry for 5 minutes on each side.

Recommended with: Make 1 batch of the Za'atar Dressing (see **Salads and Dressings**), add half a 12 oz. box of Mori-Nu silken tofu to thicken the dressing, and this essentially creates a Za'atar Aioli.

Crabby Sea Cakes, aka Vegan Crabby Patties

Similar to my Ocean House Salad, I'm hesitant to call this a vegan crab cake. I've never had a crab cake before, so I can't say what it tastes like, and anyway to call it a crab cake would probably be setting up unfair expectations. It's its own thing, a veggie patty that uses dulse seaweed flakes to give it a sea flavor; I love this for what it is but also for what it isn't.

MAKES 8 PATTIES

One 14 oz. can organic hearts of palm, roughly chopped
One 14 oz. block of extra-firm tofu (pressed for 30 minutes to
    remove water)
½ cup eggless mayo (see **Odds and Ends**)
2 tsp dulse seaweed flakes
1 Tbsp Dijon mustard
1 tsp Old Bay Seasoning
1 tsp celery salt
1 tsp dried parsley, or 1 Tbsp fresh chopped parsley
½ tsp sriracha
½ cup Panko bread crumbs

Add the hearts of palm and tofu to a food processor and pulse until the mixture is crumbled. Add to a mixing bowl with the remaining ingredients except the bread crumbs and stir until combined, then cover and refrigerate for 30 minutes. Remove the mixture and form eight patties, then coat the sides of each patty in bread crumbs and panfry 5 minutes on each side.

Note: Tartar sauce is similar to my recipe for Thousand Island Dressing (see **Salads and Dressings**). Make a batch of the Thousand Island Dressing, but leave out the French dressing / ketchup, and once the ingredients are blended, add 1 tsp minced capers and 1 tsp minced fresh parsley (or dried), and mix together.

Thai Veggie Burgers

This recipe features the Thai trifecta of lime, lemongrass, and ginger in veggie burger form for a unique and tasty experience.

MAKES 6 PATTIES

1½ cups cooked chickpeas
½ cup cooked sweet potato
½ cup quick oats
⅓ cup roasted peanuts, unsalted
¼ cup fresh cilantro
1 tsp powdered ginger
1 tsp garlic powder
1" stalk lemongrass
Juice of 1 lime
1 tsp sea salt
¼ tsp chili powder

Combine all ingredients in a food processor and pulse until the ingredients are chopped well but not pureed. Let the mixture set for 20 minutes, then form into patty shapes and panfry on each side for 5 minutes.

Recommended with: Massaman Curry Sauce or Thai Peanut Sauce (see **Bowls and Sauces**), or combine Eggless Mayo (see **Odds and Ends**) with 1 tsp store-bought red curry paste.

Vegan Corned Beef Hash Burger

So many of the flavors we're used to is really the blend of spices used, and this recipe is a great example of that.

MAKES 6 PATTIES

½ medium red onion, finely chopped
½ cup frozen corn
¼ tsp liquid smoke
1 tsp garlic powder
1 tsp sea salt
2 cups of ground Vegan Corned Beef (see **Odds and Ends**)
1 medium Russet potato, peeled, cubed, and cooked until
       fork-tender
1 cup cornmeal

In a small skillet, sauté the onion and corn with the liquid smoke, garlic powder, and sea salt until the onion is translucent.

Add the skillet ingredients, Vegan Corned Beef, and cooked potato to a food processor, and pulse until the ingredients are well combined. Shape the mixture into six patties, and in a plate or shallow bowl coat each side of the patties with cornmeal, and panfry for 5 minutes on each side.

Recommended with: Use potato rolls, topped with the shredded green cabbage and Swiss Cheese Sauce (see **Odds and Ends**) spread on both halves of the bun.

Italian-Style Vegan Meatballs

I like to make large batches of these Italian-Style Vegan Meatballs and freeze them so I have some on-hand for when I need to throw together some quick pasta and sauce for the boys.

MAKES 12 BALLS

2 Tbsp chia seeds
½ cup water
Half a 15 oz. package extra-firm tofu, pressed and mashed
½ cup panko bread crumbs
4 sundried tomatoes, soaked and chopped
¼ cup fresh basil, chopped
1 Tbsp nutritional yeast
1 tsp Better Than Bouillon, No Beef flavor
1 tsp dried oregano
½ tsp garlic powder
½ tsp onion powder
½ tsp ground fennel seeds
½ tsp ground black pepper
½ cup vital wheat gluten

Using a spice grinder, grind the chia seeds until it's essentially a powder, then combine with the ½ cup of water, whisk together, then set aside for 10 minutes.

Add the tofu, bread crumbs, sundried tomatoes, and basil to a metal mixing bowl with the seasonings, and mix together. Add the chia seed mixture to the bowl and mix well.

Finally, add the wheat gluten, and mix together with your hands. Let the mixture sit for 10 minutes, then form into meatballs.

If using an air fryer, spray the meatballs with cooking spray and cook for 6 minutes at 370° F, then remove and shake the pan, spray the meatballs, and cook for an additional 6 minutes. Alternatively, you can panfry the meatballs in a non-stick pan.

These Italian-Style Vegan Meatballs should hold up well in a sauce, but they are already cooked at this point, so you can pour a sauce such as the Sun Dried Tomato Marinara Sauce (see **Bowls and Sauces**) over the meatballs; there is no need to simmer the meatballs in the sauce to cook them further.

Porcupine Meatballs

This recipe is based on one of my favorite dishes I had growing up, which was made with ground beef and pieces of rice sticking out of the meatballs like spines (hence the name Porcupine Meatballs), cooked in a creamy tomato soup base. After many failed attempts, I have finally managed to crack the code and veganize one of my favorite childhood dishes—so delicious!

MAKES 10 BALLS

2 Tbsp ground chia seeds
1 Tbsp Better Than Bouillon, No Beef flavor
1 cup water
1 medium green pepper, finely chopped
1 medium yellow onion, finely chopped
4 cloves garlic, crushed
One 8 oz. block tempeh, crumbled in a food processor
1 cup cooked long-grain brown rice
½ tsp ground black pepper
1 cup vital wheat gluten
1 batch Creamy Tomato Soup

Add the ground chia seeds, bouillon, and water to a pint Mason jar or small container, shake well, and set aside for 10 minutes, shaking every few minutes to make sure the water absorbs evenly.

Water-sauté the green pepper, onion, and garlic until soft. Add to a large mixing bowl along with the crumbled tempeh, brown rice, and black pepper. Mix well. Add the chia mixture and stir into the mixing bowl. Add the wheat gluten and mix together with your hands until the ingredients are well combined. Let the mixture set for 10 minutes, then form the mixture into 2" balls. Use cooking spray to coat the meatballs, then bake at 325°F for 30 minutes on a non-stick baking sheet.

In an 8" x 8" casserole dish, add 1 batch of the Creamy Tomato Soup recipe (see **Souper Soups**), but only use 5 tomatoes in the soup recipe instead of 10; then add the meatballs to the casserole dish. Cover the casserole dish with aluminum foil and bake for 15 minutes at 350° F, remove and stir the meatballs, and return to bake for another 15 minutes.

Swedish-Style Vegan Meatballs

These vegan meatballs are a welcome addition to mushroom stroga-noff or added to bowl meals.

MAKES 12 BALLS

1 medium yellow onion, finely chopped
2 Tbsp + 2 tsp chia seeds
½ cup water
Half a 15 oz. block of extra-firm tofu, pressed and mashed
½ cup panko bread crumbs
1 tsp sea salt
½ tsp ground nutmeg
½ tsp ground allspice
½ tsp ground black pepper
½ cup vital wheat gluten

Water-sauté the chopped onion until soft.

Using a spice grinder, grind the chia seeds until it's essentially a powder, then combine with the ½ cup of water and whisk together, then set aside for 10 minutes.

In a large metal mixing bowl mash the tofu, then add the sautéed onions, bread crumbs, and seasonings, and mix together. Add the chia seed mixture to the bowl and mix well. Finally, add the wheat gluten and mix together with your hands. Let the mixture sit for 10 minutes, then form into meatballs.

If using an air fryer, spray the meatballs with cooking spray and cook for 6 minutes at 370° F, then remove and shake the pan, spray the meatballs, and cook for an additional 6 minutes. Alternatively, you can panfry the meatballs in a non-stick pan. These Vegan Swedish Meatballs should hold up well in a sauce, but they are already cooked at this point, so you can pour a sauce such as the Stroganoff Sauce (see **Bowls and Sauces**) over the meatballs; there is no need to simmer the meatballs in the sauce to cook them further.

Note: Ground chia seeds are used in this recipe as a binder because it has a more neutral taste, and also because ground flax seeds have a distinctive texture that is distracting in baked goods or in vegan meatballs such as these.

Vegan Reuben Sandwich

Admittedly, this recipe doesn't necessarily belong in this chapter, as it's not really a burger per se, but I'm going to exercise my author's privileges and include it here since a good vegan Reuben sandwich is a thing of beauty, and it doesn't take that much of a switch of ingredients to turn the Vegan Corned Beef Hash Burger recipe into a delicious Vegan Reuben. It's too good not to include, but it does take some planning and time to put together.

MAKES 1 SANDWICH

2 "sausages" of the Vegan Corned Beef recipe (see **Odds and Ends**)
2 Tbsp Swiss Cheese Sauce (see **Odds and Ends**)
¼ cup sauerkraut
2 slices of toasted rye bread
2 Tbsp Thousand Island Dressing (see **Salads and Dressings**)

Follow the recipe for making the Vegan Corned Beef recipe, but instead of using the food processor to make crumbles from the cooked sausage shapes, just slice the sausages thinly for this sandwich. Spread the Swiss Cheese Sauce on both pieces of bread, add the Vegan Corned Beef, and spread the Thousand Island Dressing over it, then finish assembling the sandwich. Enjoy!

Nine Types of Fries

Because in a chapter of veggie burgers, the natural pairing would be a side of crispy fries! Here is a tasty assortment of choices if you want to try moving beyond the basic potato. These recipes call for using an air fryer, but if you want to bake them in the oven that works too—just place them on a non-stick baking mat on a baking sheet, and you may need to extend the baking time somewhat until the fries are cooked through.

1. **French Fries:** Use a fry cutter on 2 medium Russet or gold potatoes, toss with ½ tsp garlic powder, ½ tsp salt, and 1 tsp oil. Air-fry for 12 minutes at 370° F, shake basket, and bake for 12 more minutes. (makes approximately 2 cups)

2. **Sweet Potato Fries:** Peel 2 medium sweet potatoes and use a fry cutter, toss with 1 tsp oil and ½ tsp salt, air-fry for 10 minutes at 370° F, shake basket, and bake for 10 more minutes. Serve with Carolina Gold Sauce. (makes approximately 2 cups)

3. **Carrot Stick Fries:** Cut 3 large carrots into ¼" sticks and toss with 1 tsp oil, ½ tsp smoked paprika, ½ tsp salt, and 1 tsp maple syrup. Air-fry for 8 minutes at 370, shake basket, and bake for 8 more minutes. (makes approximately 1 ½ cups)

4. **Polenta Fries:** Cut a polenta tube in half, use fry cutter, and toss with ½ tsp salt, 1 tsp oil, ½ tsp ground rosemary, and ½ tsp garlic powder. Air-fry for 10 minutes at 370° F, shake basket, and bake for 10 more minutes. (makes approximately 1 ½ cups)

5. **Jicama Fries:** Peel and cut half of a large jicama root into ¼" strips, and toss with ½ tsp salt, 1 tsp oil, and 1 tsp maple

syrup. Air-fry for 10 minutes at 370° F, shake basket, and bake for 10 more minutes. (makes approximately 1 ½ cups)

6. **We Got the Beet Fries:** Peel 3 large beets, use a fry cutter, and toss with ½ tsp ground thyme, ½ tsp garlic powder, 1 tsp oil, and ½ tsp salt. Air-fry for 8 minutes at 370° F, shake basket, and bake for 8 more minutes. (makes approximately 1 ½ cups)

7. **Celeriac Fries:** Peel and cut medium celeriac root into ¼" strips, toss with ½ tsp salt and 1 tsp oil, air-fry for 10 minutes at 400° F, shake basket, and bake for 10 more minutes. (makes approximately 1 ½ cups)

8. **Skewered Onion Fries:** Use a fry cutter on a large yellow onion to start, then add wooden skewers to each fry stack, cut onion all the way through, and cut the skewer end to shorten it. In a small mixing bowl combine 2 Tbsp all-purpose flour, 1 tsp salt, ½ tsp ground pepper, and ½ cup vegan liquid egg mixture. Dredge the skewered onions in the liquid mixture, then add in a bowl of 1 cup panko breadcrumbs to cover, then air-fry 450° F for 6 minutes, remove, and shake. Cook for 8 more minutes. (makes approximately 1 cup)

9. **Plantain Fries:** Peel and slice a large green plantain down the middle, then slice into wedges. Toss with 1 Tbsp molasses, 1 tsp coriander, ½ tsp sea salt, and 1 tsp oil. Air-fry for 8 minutes at 400° F, remove, and shake. Cook for 8 more minutes. (makes approximately 1 cup)

On A Casserole

Can a casserole be any good without layers of cheese and ground meat? Just watch how quickly the Kid's Favorite Lasagna disappears in my house! Bring the Lean and Mean Green Bean Casserole for Thanksgiving and nobody's going to care if it's healthy! This chapter features recipes for large-quantity meals, perfect to share with a group or for making lunch for a week.

On a Casserole as a System

I'm not going to deny it, these recipes take some time to make, but it's what you do with them once they're cooked that makes all the difference. I mean, besides eating it.

It's time to break out the glass storage containers; I like to cut these casseroles up and put them into single-sized, square glass storage containers, which are easy to grab and go for lunch, or make a quick dinner. They heat up quickly in the oven or the microwave once they're defrosted. This makes large batch-meals like casseroles easy to store, and keeping them in individual single-serving containers keeps the portions easier to manage. Trust me, these recipes are so good it will be tempting to eat the whole thing, so break up the party and you can enjoy the fruits of your cooking efforts for days to come!

On A Casserole

Rice Nut Pie

This recipe comes straight from my mother's kitchen, admittedly it's not one that I liked much as a child but fell in love with as I got older. This is a delicious combination of fragrant rice, fresh herbs, and chopped nuts!

MAKES 8 SERVINGS

1 cup brown basmati rice
1 cup short-grain brown rice
2 bay leaves
½ tsp sea salt
1 Tbsp tomato paste
3½ cups water
1 cup raw walnuts
1 cup raw almonds
¼ cup chopped fresh mint
½ cup chopped parsley
3 cloves garlic
Juice of 1 lemon
Remainder of 6 oz. can tomato paste

In a large saucepan, dry-roast both types of rice for several minutes, stirring constantly, until it begins to smell nutty. Add the bay leaves, salt, tomato paste, and water, and stir until the tomato paste is dissolved. Bring to a simmer, then cover and cook for 30–40 minutes, until the water is absorbed.

While the rice mixture is cooking, add the nuts, mint, parsley, and garlic to a food processor and blend until all the ingredients are well combined, stopping the food processor several times to scrape down the sides.

In a large metal mixing bowl, add the mixture from the food processor with the lemon juice. When the rice is done cooking, remove the bay leaves and add to the contents of the mixing bowl. Stir the contents together well, then pour and pack down into a ceramic pie plate. Spread the remaining tomato paste across the top of the mixture, spreading out evenly using the back of a spoon. Bake in the oven at 350° F for 15 minutes.

Kid's Favorite Lasagna

If my boys had their way, I would make this lasagna for them at least once a week!

MAKES 12 SERVINGS

1 box lasagna noodles (you can use standard lasagna noodles, they don't have to be no-bake)

FOR THE WHITE SAUCE:
1⅓ cup raw cashews
⅔ cup water
⅓ cup nutritional yeast
Juice of ½ lemon
2 Tbsp tapioca starch
1 small shallot
1 clove garlic
1 tsp sea salt

FOR THE TOMATO SAUCE:
5 medium tomatoes
1 medium yellow onion, roughly chopped
2 carrots, unpeeled and roughly chopped
2 stalks celery, roughly chopped
1 red bell pepper, roughly chopped
3 cloves garlic
1 tsp sea salt
2 cups frozen spinach, thawed and pressed
½ cup fresh basil, chopped

2 cups Vegan Ground "Meat" Crumbles (see **Odds and Ends**)
2 medium zucchini, peeled and sliced lengthwise into ⅛" strips
Parmesan-Like Topping (see **Odds and Ends**)

In a high-powered blender, combine the ingredients for the white sauce and blend until smooth. Pour into a small mixing bowl and set aside.

Add the tomato sauce ingredients to the blender and blend until smooth. In a large mixing bowl, add the blended tomato sauce ingredients with the spinach and basil. Mix well and set aside.

Preheat the oven to 425° F. In a baking dish, add 1 cup tomato sauce first, then add a layer of uncooked lasagna noodles, a layer of zucchini slices, and 1 cup of the white sauce. Add the Vegan Ground "Meat" Crumbles, then layers of red sauce, lasagna noodles, white sauce, zucchini slices, and the rest of the tomato sauce. Top with 1 cup of the Parmesan-Like Topping, cover with aluminum foil, and bake for 60 minutes.

Note: If you want to eliminate the lasagna noodles from this recipe, I recommend using more layers of zucchini slices instead.

Curry Vegetable Pot Pie

This recipe is a fun and tasty alternative to traditional pot pies, with a curry twist.

MAKES 12 SERVINGS

Half a 15 oz. block extra-firm tofu, sliced into small cubes
2 cups chopped mushrooms
1 cup Yukon Gold potatoes, chopped into small cubes
1 large yellow onion, chopped
2 large carrots, peeled (save the peels) and cut into ¼" thick
      rounds
1 cup peas (frozen is fine)

FOR THE SAUCE:
1 cup hot water
½ cup raw cashews
½ cup coconut manna / butter
Peels of the carrots and potatoes
2 Tbsp all-purpose flour
1 Tbsp Blasphemous Curry Powder (see **Odds and Ends**)
1 tsp Better Than Bouillon, No Chicken flavor
1 sheet frozen puff pastry, thawed

Press the tofu for 15 minutes to squeeze out the excess water. Meanwhile, chop the mushrooms, cube the potatoes (keep the peels), and then cube the tofu. Water-sauté the mushrooms, onion, and carrots in a large skillet or saucepan, then add the tofu, potatoes, and peas, and remove from heat.

In a high-powered blender, combine the sauce ingredients and blend until completely smooth. Pour the sauce into the saucepan with the other ingredients. Simmer for 5 minutes, then pour the mixture into a 9" x 13" casserole dish. Cut the sheet of puff pastry into 3" squares and add each square side-by-side on top of the mixture in the casserole dish. Brush the tops of the squares of pastry, and bake for 20 minutes at 425° F.

Lean and Mean Green Bean Casserole

This is one of my favorite dishes to make at Thanksgiving, but why wait for the holiday? This recipe will make everyone want to eat their green beans and ask for more.

MAKES 8 SERVINGS

4 cups fresh green beans, cut into 3" long segments
2 cups button mushrooms, roughly chopped
1 poblano pepper, seeded and diced
Several dashes liquid smoke

FOR THE SAUCE:
1 cup water
1 cup raw cashews
1 Tbsp tamari
1 Tbsp Better Than Bouillon, Mushroom flavor
½ tsp ground black pepper
1 tsp sea salt

FOR THE CRISPY FRIED ONIONS:
1 large yellow onion, roughly chopped, or 1 ½ cups shallots sliced
        into rings
6 Tbsp panko bread crumbs
1 Tbsp all-purpose flour
1 Tbsp water
1 tsp vegetable oil

⅔ cup Bacony Vegan Bits (see **Odds and Ends**)

Steam the green beans for 10 minutes, then add to a large mixing bowl. While the beans are steaming, add the mushrooms and poblano pepper to a food processor with an "S" blade, and pulse until chopped well. Water-sauté the mushroom-pepper mixture for several minutes with a few dashes of liquid smoke until the mushrooms are soft. Add to the mixing bowl with the green beans and stir.

In a high-powered blender, combine the sauce ingredients and blend until well combined. Pour the sauce into the large mixing bowl and stir. Pour the mixture into a casserole dish, cover with aluminum foil, and bake for 30 minutes at 375° F.

Combine the ingredients for the crispy fried onions together into a separate mixing bowl, toss, and cook in an air fryer for 8 minutes on 370° F.

Remove the basket, shake well, and cook for another 8 minutes at 370° F. Alternatively, spread out over parchment paper or silicone baking mat on a rimmed baking sheet, and bake in the oven on a lower rack with the casserole for 8 minutes, then remove to the mixing bowl, add another 1 tsp oil, toss, then bake for another 8 minutes.

Remove the foil, spread the crispy fried onions and Bacony Vegan Bits over the casserole, and return to the oven for an additional 10 minutes before serving.

Vegan Cottage Pie

If you're making Shepherd's Pie with anything besides lamb or mutton (Who is looking at a lamb and thinking that would taste great, anyway? Cartoon villains, that's who.), it is technically considered a Cottage Pie. So let lambs be lambs instead of dinner, and fill up your Cottage Pie with healthy and hearty ingredients!

MAKES 12 SERVINGS

FOR THE POTATOES:
2 pounds Yukon Gold or yellow potatoes
⅓ cup peeled cloves garlic
1 tsp sea salt
⅓ cup cashew cream
½ tsp ground black pepper

FOR THE FILLING:
1½ cups Vegan Ground "Meat" Crumbles (see Odds and Ends)
1½ cups cooked brown lentils
1 medium yellow onion, finely chopped
1 large carrot, peeled and finely chopped
2 stalks celery, finely chopped
1 cup peas (can use frozen)
2 medium tomatoes, pureed
1 tsp Better Than Bouillon, No Beef flavor
1 tsp dried thyme
1 tsp sea salt
1 tsp ground pepper

Wash the potatoes, peel half of them, and cut into 1" cubes. Place the potatoes, garlic, and salt in a large saucepan with water to cover by 1 inch. Bring to a boil, then lower to medium-low and cover for 30–40 minutes until the potatoes are soft. Drain the potatoes, but save the cooking water. Add the cashew cream to the potatoes and slowly add the cooking water back in small amounts, and mash the potatoes until creamy. Stir in the black pepper, cover, and set aside.

Stir-fry the Vegan Ground "Meat" Crumbles for 5 minutes in a cast-iron skillet. In a large mixing bowl, add the filling ingredients including the crumbles and stir together. In a 9" x 13" casserole dish, pour in the filling ingredients, then spread the mashed potatoes over the mixture. Bake at 375° F for 20 minutes covered with aluminum foil, then remove the foil and bake for an additional 10 minutes before serving.

Gold and Orange Scalloped Potatoes

Cheesy, creamy sliced potatoes. It's hard to go wrong with this one!

MAKES 8 SERVINGS

3 cups Yukon Gold potatoes, peeled (save skins) and sliced into
⅛" rounds
2 cups sweet potatoes, peeled and sliced into ⅛" rounds
1 medium yellow onion, sliced into ⅛" rounds

FOR THE SAUCE:
2 cups water
⅔ cup raw cashews
Peels from the potatoes
⅓ cup nutritional yeast
3 Tbsp all-purpose flour
2 tsp Nutiva vegan butter flavoring (optional)
1 tsp dry mustard
2 tsp sea salt
1 tsp turmeric powder
½ tsp ground black pepper
1 Tbsp fresh thyme leaves, finely minced (or use ¾ tsp dried
thyme)

Slice the all of the potatoes into thin rounds using a knife or a mandoline, mix, and set aside.

Slice the onion into thin slices using a knife or a mandoline, and set aside.

In a high-powered blender, combine all sauce ingredients except the thyme and blend until completely smooth. Add the thyme leaves to the blender container and mix in with a spoon (do not turn on blender to mix).

In a 9" x 13" baking dish, pour enough of the sauce to cover the bottom of the casserole dish. Add a layer of potatoes, then a layer of onions, and pour a cup of the sauce to cover. Add another layer of potatoes, a layer of onions, then pour the remaining sauce over the casserole and cover with aluminum foil. Bake at 400° F for 60 minutes, remove foil and reduce heat to 350° F, and bake for an additional 10 minutes.

Roasted Red Pepper Mini Quiches

These bite-sized tasty treats are great to bring to parties and share with friends!

MAKES 12 SERVINGS

Oil-Free Savory Crust (see **Odds and Ends**)
One 15 oz. box of firm tofu
½ cup cashew cream
¼ cup nutritional yeast
1 tsp sea salt (use black salt if you have it)
½ tsp turmeric powder
¼ tsp garlic powder, onion powder, mustard powder
1 roasted red bell pepper, finely chopped
1 cup broccoli (frozen is fine), finely chopped
Smoked paprika for topping

You can use a muffin pan to make these mini quiches, or use mini-tart pans. If you are using a muffin pan, roll out the dough for the crust and cut circles the same size as the bottom of the muffin cups. If you are using mini-tart pans, cut circles slightly larger than the circumference of the mini-tarts and press the dough in place to cover the bottom and sides. For either type of pan, make sure to use cooking spray to coat the pan first before adding the dough to prevent it from sticking. Bake the crust for 7 minutes at 425° F, then remove and let cool.

In a large mixing bowl, use a potato masher to crumble the tofu, then add the remaining ingredients and mix together well. Spoon the mixture onto the crusts until the muffin cups or mini-tarts are filled, then sprinkle with smoked paprika. Bake the mini-quiches for 30 minutes at 350° F.

Super Stuffed Shells

Who doesn't love a casserole dish full of stuffed shells? The tangy tofu ricotta and fresh tomato sauce with basil will make it hard to stop putting more on your plate.

MAKES 12 SERVINGS

12 oz. box of jumbo shells

FOR THE MARINARA SAUCE:
10 medium tomatoes, diced
1 medium onion, diced
3 cloves garlic
¼ cup balsamic vinegar
1 Tbsp agave nectar or maple syrup
1 tsp sea salt
½ cup fresh basil, chopped

FOR THE RICOTTA:
One 15oz. block firm tofu (not extra-firm)
2 Italian-Style Vegan Sausages (see **Odds and Ends**), chopped
½ cup fresh parsley
½ cup raw cashews
½ cup water
Juice of ½ lemon
¼ cup nutritional yeast
1 cup frozen spinach, thawed and pressed
1 tsp sea salt

Cook shells until almost done, drain, and cover with cold water
    While the shells are cooking, dice the tomatoes and add to a large fine-mesh strainer over a mixing bowl, and let stand for

15 minutes to drain out some of the liquid from the tomatoes. In a large saucepan, water-sauté the onions and garlic until the onions are soft, then add the tomatoes, balsamic vinegar, agave, and sea salt. Use a potato masher to press break up the tomatoes further. Simmer the mixture for 5 minutes, then stir in the basil, and remove from heat.

Press the tofu for 15 minutes, then slice into three slabs and pat each with paper towels until dry. Break up and add to a food processor with the sausage and parsley, and blend until crumbled. In a high-speed blender, combine the cashews, water, and lemon juice until pureed, then pour into a large mixing bowl with the food processor mixture, add nutritional yeast, thawed spinach, and salt, and stir to combine.

Add 1 cup of the marinara to the bottom of a 9" x 13" baking dish. Scoop the ricotta mixture into each of the shells until they are filled, and line the shells up in the baking dish. Once you have a layer of shells, cover them with the remaining marinara sauce. Cover with foil and bake for at 375° F for 25 minutes. Remove foil, and bake another 15 minutes.

Layered Hash Brown and Tofu Scramble

If there's one recipe I've made over and over throughout the years, tweaking it until it's just right, it's tofu scramble. Hash browns and fresh tomato salsa are a winning combination.

MAKES 8 SERVINGS

FOR THE HASH BROWNS:
3 cups water
1 large russet potato, peeled
1 medium yellow onion
1 tsp sea salt
½ tsp liquid smoke
1 tsp oil

FOR THE TOFU SCRAMBLE:
One 14 oz. block of firm tofu
1 tsp turmeric powder
1 tsp black salt, or sea salt
1 tsp garlic powder
1 tsp ground black pepper
⅓ cup nutritional yeast
¼ cup water
1 cup frozen spinach, thawed and pressed
1 tsp oil

FOR THE FRESH SALSA:
1 medium tomato, finely chopped
1 Tbsp finely chopped yellow onion
1 Tbsp fresh cilantro, chopped
Juice of ½ lime
1 tsp sriracha
¼ tsp garlic powder
¼ tsp sea salt

For the hash browns, use a box grater to grate the potatoes over a large mixing bowl with several cups of water. Once the potato is fully grated, run your hand through the water and rinse the potato, then strain the water. Use the box grater to grate the onion, and combine with the grated potato. Spread the mixture out on a cloth towel or paper towels, roll up the towel, and squeeze to remove as much moisture as possible. Stir in the mixing bowl with salt and liquid smoke. Heat 1 tsp oil in a non-stick pan and add the potato/onion mixture and pat down to compress. Cook on medium-low for 15 minutes uncovered, then flip the hash brown and add another 1 tsp of cooking oil to help prevent sticking, and cook for an additional 15 minutes.

For the tofu scramble, drain the tofu, then break it up with a knife and use a potato masher to mash the tofu into crumbles in a skillet. Add 1 tsp cooking oil, turmeric, salt, garlic powder, and black pepper. Cook on medium heat for 5 minutes, stirring frequently. Add the nutritional yeast and water and stir well to make sure the nutritional yeast is mixed in. Add the frozen spinach and stir to combine, then cover for several minutes. Remove the cover and stir, then cover for several more minutes, then shut off the heat and uncover.

For the fresh salsa, add the salsa ingredients to mixing bowl and stir to combine.

In a casserole dish, break up the hash browns and place as the bottom layer, then cover with the tofu scramble. Add top layer of fresh salsa, and slice into portions to serve. If you want to freeze the hash brown and tofu scramble to reheat later, it's best to make the salsa fresh and top it before eating, as the salsa won't freeze well.

Russian Hybrid Stuffed Bell Peppers

In this recipe, I've added the filling from Russian stuffed cabbage leaves into colorful bell peppers, which lets you enjoy the taste of delicious cabbage rolls without all the work of boiling and rolling the cabbage leaves.

MAKES 12 SERVINGS

FOR THE SAUCE:
5 medium tomatoes, roughly chopped
2 Medjool dates
2 Tbsp apple cider vinegar
1 tsp sea salt

6 bell peppers (red, yellow, and green)
2 cups Vegan Ground "Meat" Crumbles (see **Odds and Ends**)
1½ cups cooked buckwheat groats
1 cup green cabbage, finely shredded and chopped
1 large yellow onion, minced
3 cloves garlic, crushed
2 tsp sea salt
1 tsp ground black pepper

In a high-powered blender, add the tomatoes, dates, apple cider vinegar, and salt and blend until completely pureed.

Cut a thin layer from the bottom of each bell pepper so that it can stand upright (cut just enough so that there are several small holes at the bottom of each pepper), and cut away the tops of each pepper so that the tops are intact and set aside; remove the seeds and stem. In a large mixing bowl, combine the Vegan Ground "Meat" Crumbles, buckwheat, cabbage, onion, garlic, salt, and black pepper with 1 cup of the tomato sauce.

Pour enough of the tomato sauce to cover the bottom of a 9" x 13" casserole dish, then add the bell peppers. Stuff each of the peppers with the filling until mostly full, then pour some tomato sauce on top of each pepper and place the cut-away tops back on. Pour the remainder of the sauce around the base of the peppers. Cover the dish with aluminum foil and bake for 30 minutes at 350° F, then remove the foil and bake for an additional 25 minutes.

Baked Mac and Cheez Casserole

We're going to put a healthy spin on one of my favorite casseroles from my (and a lot of people's) childhood: the gooey, cheesy Baked Mac and Cheez Casserole. And we can keep the delicious decadence without all the fat.

MAKES 12 SERVINGS

4 cups cooked macaroni or shells (whole-grain or rice pasta if possible)
1 batch of Super-Creamy Alfredo Sauce (see **Bowls and Sauces**)
6 Tbsp tapioca starch
2 Roma tomatoes, roughly chopped
1 medium red onion, roughly chopped

FOR THE TOPPING:
1½ cups panko bread crumbs, or 1 cup panko bread crumbs with 1 cup crispy fried onions

Cook the pasta according to directions on the box until al-dente. While the pasta is cooking, make a batch of the Super-Creamy Alfredo Sauce, with the addition of the tapioca starch. In a food processor, blend the tomatoes and onion until pureed. Once the pasta is done cooking, mix the pasta, sauce, and the tomato/onion mixture together and stir until well combined. Pour the mixture into a casserole dish and cover with the topping. Bake in the oven for 30 minutes at 375° F.

Note: If you want to use just the panko bread crumbs as a topping, spraying the bread crumbs before baking will make them brown and crispier.

ChickSea Casserole

The idea of this recipe is similar to tuna casserole, but it's something you'd actually want to eat!

MAKES 9 SERVINGS

FOR THE SAUCE:
½ cup raw cashews
1 cup water
⅓ cup nutritional yeast
Juice of ½ lemon
3 Tbsp tapioca starch
1 tsp Better Than Bouillon
1 tsp dulse flakes

FOR THE FILLING:
2½ cups cooked chickpeas
½ medium red onion
2 stalks celery
1 spear dill pickle
½ tsp sea salt
½ tsp Old Bay Seasoning
1½ tsp dulse flakes

One 18 oz. tube organic polenta
2 large tomatoes, diced

Blend the sauce ingredients together in a high-powered blender for several minutes until well combined.

In a food processor, combine the filling ingredients and pulse until the ingredients are chopped and broken down. Do not process to the point that it creates a paste; the idea is just to chop the ingredients into small pieces.

Slice the polenta into ¼" rounds. Coat the bottom of an 8" x 8" pan with cooking spray and pour a thin layer of sauce in the bottom of the pan, then add a layer of polenta, covered by a layer of filling. Use a fork to press the filling down so that it's not loose. Add a layer of diced tomatoes, then pour a layer of sauce on top. Add another layer of polenta, then filling, and cover with the remaining sauce. Press in a layer of diced tomatoes as a top layer, then bake in the oven for 30 minutes at 400° F.

Unconventional Moussaka

I may be flouting convention here, but let's take a pass on the ground beef or lamb and use healthy, whole-food ingredients instead.

MAKES 12 SERVINGS

FOR THE VEGGIES:
10 Japanese eggplants sliced into ¼" thick rounds

FOR THE GROUND "MEAT" FILLING:
1½ cups Vegan Ground "Meat" Crumbles (see **Odds and Ends**)
1 medium red onion, finely chopped
2 cloves garlic, crushed
2 medium tomatoes, finely chopped
½ cup dry red wine

½ bunch of fresh parsley, chopped
⅔ cup uncooked brown lentils
½ tsp ground cinnamon
½ tsp ground nutmeg

FOR THE SAUCE:
1½ cups water
½ cup raw cashews
1 medium Russet potato, roughly chopped
2 cloves garlic
1 tsp sea salt
2 green olives, pitted
½ tsp turmeric powder

Slice the eggplants (unpeeled) into 1" thick rounds. Spray a baking sheet with cooking spray and lay the eggplant rounds out in one layer, and spray again to cover, then broil briefly in the oven until the eggplants are golden and crispy. Remove and flip the eggplant slices, and broil briefly again until the other sides are the same, then remove.

Add the ground crumbles to a large saucepan with the onions and garlic and sauté for about 5 minutes until the crumbles are cooked and the onions are soft. Add the chopped tomatoes, wine, parsley, brown lentils, cinnamon and nutmeg, then cover and simmer for 30 minutes.

In a high-powered blender, add the sauce ingredients and blend until completely smooth.

Spray the bottom and sides of a 9" x 13" casserole dish with cooking spray, then add a layer of eggplant slices, cover with a layer of crumble filling. Add another layer of eggplant slices, another layer of crumble filling, and then cover with the sauce completely. Bake for 35 minutes at 350° F and let stand 15 minutes before serving.

Vegan Hybrid Kibbeh

I wrote this recipe as a hybrid of one delicious meal I love—kibbeh—with a layer of tangy spinach filling similar to what you'd find in a traditional spinach hand pie. The result is something new and hearty!

MAKES 9 CUPS

2 cups uncooked bulgur

4 cups water

1 small yellow onion, minced

2 Tbsp fresh flat-leaf parsley, chopped

1 Tbsp fresh mint, chopped

½ tsp Seven Spices mixture (see **Odds and Ends**)

½ tsp ground black pepper

¼ tsp ground cinnamon

1 tsp sea salt

¼ cup pine nuts

2 cups Vegan Ground "Meat" Crumbles (see **Odds and Ends**)

2 cups frozen spinach, thawed and pressed

Juice of 1 lemon

4 Tbsp finely chopped yellow onion

1 Tbsp sumac

½ tsp garlic powder

½ tsp sea salt

Add the bulgur to a large saucepan with the water and bring to a boil, then turn to low heat and cook uncovered until the water evaporates, about 15 minutes. Remove from the burner and let cool. Add the mixture to a large mixing bowl with the remaining ingredients through Ground "Meat" Crumbles, and mix well by hand. In a separate small mixing bowl, combine the spinach and remaining ingredients, and mix together.

In an 8"x8" casserole dish, spray the bottom of the pan with cooking spray and add half of the bulgur/crumble mixture and press into the bottom of the pan. Spread the spinach mixture over the bulgur/crumble mixture, then add another layer of the remaining bulgur/crumble mixture. Bake at 350° F uncovered for 35–40 minutes.

Bowls and Sauces

For me, a good sauce is the key to eating a whole-food, plant-based diet. It's like the fairy dust of the healthy food world: serve up some whole grains, beans, and veggies, and a delicious sauce magically transforms it from boring into fantastic!

Not long ago, I stopped in at a cafe and ordered their vegan bowl meal to go: quinoa, pinto beans, steamed beets, carrots, and kale.

When I opened the to-go container, I actually turned around and went back in, asking, "Is there a sauce that's supposed to go with this?" Nope, that's how it is. I thought to myself, *That's not a meal; that's a punishment*, and I guess my expression said it all because the server added, "We don't add any sauce because then it wouldn't be healthy." I guess she was right, if by sauce she meant a mayo or oil-based sauce that's like a liquid fat bomb. But *it doesn't have to be like that*. The power of sauce is that it can magically transform a meal from a punishment into something you want a second helping of. That's how I get my boys to eat so many whole grains, beans, and, yes, even kale.

Just like in the **Salads and Dressings** section, cashews play an important role in many of these recipes in replacing oil. For years, I made the Golden Cheezy Sauce as a roux, mixing flour and vegan butter first. Once I learned about using cashews, I replaced the butter and discovered that I couldn't tell the difference! So with the same taste and the same consistency, with only a fifth of the fat and calories, why wouldn't I just use cashews from now on? Many of these sauce recipes, like the Golden Cheezy Sauce, are what I consider to be utility sauces—it doesn't really matter what they go over, but they make the dish taste a lot better. I see many recipes for bowl meals that carefully pair different ingredients together, which you can certainly do, and I've included some suggestions in my sauce recipes, but most of these sauces can be poured over whatever combinations of whole grains, proteins like beans or tofu, and different veggies you'd like, and it will taste delicious!

Eating well does not have to be a sacrifice. My Healthy and Delicious Sauces class is one of my favorites to teach, just to see people's faces light up when they try these sauces—they can't believe how good they are! This section includes 28 sauce recipes; some you will find familiar and some may be new tastes for you, but with a different sauce recipe every day for a month, it's hard to get bored!

Bowls and Sauces as a System

These sauces can also be very convenient—make a large batch of sauce and pour it into ice cube trays (silicone trays work best) and freeze them, then store the cubes in freezer bags. Most whole grains and beans can be cooked and frozen. If you want to have bowl meals that are super quick, just heat up a few cubes of sauce over grains and beans from the freezer, and while that's heating up you can cut up and steam some veggies. In 15 minutes you can have a whole-food, plant-based meal that is incredibly healthy, tastes delicious, and will leave you full for hours.

Let the sauce be the star of the show. Ever wonder what to do with that big bunch of kale? Trying to get the kids to eat more healthy foods? Heard from a friend that you should be adding more cauliflower to your diet? When you let the sauce be the star, you'll be able to load up on kale without noticing the kale so much. Kids will ask for seconds without asking what's in it (that's what my boys do). And go ahead and throw in some fresh cauliflower florets or mix in some cauliflower "rice" with the grains (or for recipes like Super Creamy Alfredo Sauce, it's in the sauce!). The point is, using sauces can be a great way to incorporate a healthy variety of vegetables into your day!

Bowls and Sauces

Lemon Tahini Sauce

This sauce is typically what you'd find in Mediterranean or Middle Eastern restaurants with falafel, but it's actually a great utility sauce; it makes a bowl of grains, beans, and veggies taste ten times better.

MAKES 2½ CUPS

1 cup tahini
1 clove garlic
1 teaspoon grated ginger (about ½" fresh ginger)
2 Tbsp tamari
Juice of 1 lemon
1 ⅓ cup water

Place all ingredients in a high-powered blender and puree until smooth. Add more water for a thinner consistency.

Note: Tahini is ground sesame seed paste, which has a unique flavor, and the consistency is similar to peanut butter. It lasts a long time in a jar or can, so stock up when you find it at the supermarket or natural and ethnic markets

Recommended with: Quinoa, edamame, veggies, black sesame seeds.

Nacho Cheese Sauce

The cooked potatoes and cashews give this sauce a thick creaminess that you'd swear was from oil!

MAKES 4½ CUPS

2 cups diced yellow potatoes (unpeeled)
1 cup diced carrots (unpeeled)
2 cups water
3 Tbsp raw cashews
2 tsp sea salt
1 Tbsp lemon juice
½ cup nutritional yeast
¼ tsp onion powder
¼ tsp garlic powder
¼ tsp Old Bay seasoning

Boil the potatoes and carrots until soft. Drain and save the water; blend ¾ cup of the water and cashews in a high-speed blender for a minute, then add the remaining ingredients to the blender and blend on high for several minutes, continuing to add more water as needed until the sauce is creamy.

Recommended with: This sauce could be used as a nacho cheese dip, but I love to pour it over a bowl of rice and black beans, chopped tomato, sliced avocados, and some cilantro.

Cuban Smoky Sweet Sauce

A Cuban sauce like this typically has a lot of oil, sugar, and canned tomatoes, but this recipe gives it a fresh, whole-food makeover that rivals the traditional recipe.

MAKES 2½ CUPS

2 cups chopped tomatoes + 1 large tomato
2 Medjool dates
1 Tbsp raw cashews
1 large clove garlic
2 tsp tamari
1 tsp balsamic vinegar
1 tsp smoked paprika
½ tsp ground black pepper
½ tsp liquid smoke
1 tsp sea salt or to taste
¼ tsp miso paste

Place all ingredients except for the miso in a high-powered blender and puree, then add to a medium saucepan and cook for 10 minutes on medium heat. Remove from heat and stir in the miso paste.

Recommended with: Brown rice, black beans, roasted corn, green bell pepper, avocado.

Ranchero Sauce

This smoky, savory sauce is often found on huevos rancheros, but my fresh-roasted version tops off any bowl meal with a Mexican twist!

MAKES 2½ CUPS

1 red bell pepper, seeds removed
1–2 Anaheim green chilies, seeds removed
6 plum or Roma tomatoes
1 sweet white onion
3 cloves garlic, wrapped in aluminum foil
½ cup water
Juice of 1 lime
1 tsp sea salt
1 tsp Better Than Bouillon, No Chicken flavor
¼ tsp liquid smoke
¼ cup fresh cilantro, chopped

Preheat oven to 425° F. Line a rimmed baking sheet with parchment paper or a silicone baking mat. Slice the bell pepper, chilies, tomatoes, and onion in half, then place on baking sheet cut-side up with the wrapped garlic.

Bake in the oven for 10 minutes, then remove and turn the vegetables cut-side down. Return to the oven and bake for an additional 15 minutes. Remove from the oven and transfer the cooked vegetables to a food processor or blender; add the remaining ingredients and blend until smooth.

Note: You can pulse the roasted vegetables in a food processor to the consistency you like best; I prefer it smooth to get the maximum blend of flavors, but it's up to you.

Recommended with: Brown rice, pinto beans, roasted corn, avocado.

Chimichurri Sauce

Cilantro lovers rejoice! Fresh cilantro and parsley blend with lemon and spices here to create a delicious South American sauce to cover roasted vegan kebabs.

MAKES 2½ CUPS

½ cup raw cashews
½ cup water
1 cup flat-leaf parsley, minced
¼ cup fresh cilantro, minced
3 Tbsp fresh oregano, minced
Juice of 1 lemon
2 cloves garlic
½ tsp sea salt
½ tsp ground black pepper
1 small red chili pepper (optional), or 1 tsp chili pepper flakes

Blend the cashews and water for several minutes in a high-speed blender and set aside. Add the remaining ingredients to a food processor and process until well combined.

Pour the blender and sauce ingredients together into a Mason jar, cover, and shake well. The taste of the sauce will intensify if you leave the sauce unrefrigerated for several hours before serving.

Recommended with: Here's a chance to break out the skewers and make some kebabs; chimichurri sauce is frequently used as a coating on roasted or grilled meat, but I like to cover cubes of tofu or seitan with the sauce and roast it over a casserole dish with slices of bell pepper and onion. I roast the skewers until they begin to char, then add more sauce over brown rice and top with the pieces from the kebabs.

Massaman Curry Sauce

In many Thai restaurants, Massaman curry is served as more of a broth than a sauce. If you wish to thin the sauce so that it's more similar to a broth, just add some water to the saucepan.

MAKES 3 CUPS

½ cup peanut butter
¼ cup coconut manna
3 Medjool dates
2 cups water
2" stalk lemongrass
1 large shallot
3 cloves garlic
2" fresh ginger
2 kaffir lime leaves
½ tsp ground chipotle
2 Tbsp tamari
1 Tbsp tamarind paste
1 tsp ground cumin
½ tsp ground nutmeg
½ tsp ground cinnamon
½ tsp coriander
¼ tsp ground cardamom
⅛ tsp ground cloves
1 tsp salt

Blend all sauce ingredients and add to saucepan. Bring to a boil, then cover and simmer for at least 20 minutes.

Recommended with: Short-grain brown rice, tofu, sweet potato cubes, carrots, roughly chopped onion, chopped red bell pepper, topped with chopped roasted peanuts.

Note: If you want to cook carrots to go with the Massaman Curry Sauce, keep those peels! Scrub and peel the carrots before cutting, and add the peels to the blender when making the sauce.

Kaffir lime leaves can be found in Asian and natural markets fresh or in small jars; this is a specialty item that you may not use much but it's well worth seeking out (you can look online also), and it stores in the refrigerator for months.

This recipe uses a fair amount of ingredients and takes time to prepare, so this is a good sauce to double or triple, and then freeze the rest.

Pad Thai Sauce

Let's give the popular Thai noodle dish a whole-food makeover! Toss this sauce into a bowl of pad Thai noodles (or wide zucchini noodles) with fresh herbs and chopped peanuts, and enjoy a healthy meal from Southeast Asia!

MAKES 3 CUPS

2 Roma or plum tomatoes
Zest of 1 lime
Juice of 2 limes
2 clove of garlic
10 Medjool dates
1 Tbsp tamarind paste
½ cup tamari
1 medium shallot
1 Tbsp white miso

Add all ingredients except for the miso to a high-speed blender and run for 2 minutes until completely pureed.

Pour into a small saucepan and cook on medium heat for 5 minutes, then stir in the miso.

Recommended with: Pad Thai noodles, extra-firm tofu cut into ½" cubes, mung bean sprouts, chopped chives, chopped cilantro, covered with chopped roasted peanuts and sriracha.

Teriyaki Sauce

Teriyaki sauce is often used as a stir-fry sauce, but it also works well in bowl meals. Ditch the bottle of teriyaki sauce in the fridge and taste what a difference fresh, whole-food ingredients make!

MAKES 2 CUPS

½ cup tamari
½ cup mirin
½ cup water
¼ cup raw cashews
4 Medjool dates
2 tsp blackstrap molasses
1" fresh ginger
3 cloves garlic
1 ½ tsp cornstarch

Add all ingredients except the cornstarch to a high-powered blender and blend until completely smooth.

In a small saucepan, whisk the cornstarch into the sauce, and whisk the sauce for several minutes over medium heat until thickened.

Recommended with: Short-grain brown rice, edamame, sugar snap peas, steamed broccoli, chopped onions, sprinkled with sesame seeds.

Note: Mirin is a Japanese rice wine that you can find in the Asian section of supermarkets; it keeps in the pantry for months.

Sweet and Sour Sauce

This is a whole-food, oil- and sugar-free version of Chinese Sweet and Sour sauce, and as an added bonus, it's not nuclear orange....

MAKES 3 CUPS

10 Medjool dates
½ cup tamari
1 medium tomato
¼ cup apple cider vinegar
1" fresh ginger
4 tsp tahini
3 cloves garlic
1 tsp red pepper flakes (optional)
½ tsp ground black pepper
1 ½ cups frozen pineapple

Blend all ingredients together except the pineapple, and blend for a minute until well combined.

Add the pineapple and continue to blend for another minute. Pour into a small saucepan and heat on medium for 10 minutes, stirring every minute.

Recommended with: Short-grain brown rice, steamed chopped celery, green bell pepper, roasted cashews, bamboo shoots or water chestnuts, topped with sesame seeds.

Indian Yellow Lentil Curry Sauce

You might not think of lentil curry as a sauce, but it can be used as the sauce for a grain and bean bowl meal like any others in this cookbook. You can use it to spice up a variety of different vegetables, grains, and beans.

MAKES 4½ CUPS

1 medium yellow onion, diced
1 tomato, diced
2 cloves garlic
1" fresh ginger
2½ cups water
1 cup yellow lentils
½ cup red lentils
10 curry leaves
½ tsp turmeric powder
½ tsp red chili powder
1 tsp ground cumin
1 tsp ground coriander
1 ½ tsp sea salt
1 tsp Nutiva buttery coconut spread (optional)

In a large saucepan, water-sauté the onion, tomato, garlic and ginger, stirring frequently. Once the onions are soft, add the water, lentils, and curry leaves, then cover and simmer for 15 minutes. Stir in the remaining ingredients and turn off the heat. Let it sit for at least 5 minutes to let flavors mix before serving, and you can choose to remove the curry leaves if you like. If you prefer a smoother consistency, use an immersion blender in the saucepan for a minute to break down the sauce further.

Note: I highly recommend tracking down some fresh curry leaves from an Asian or natural market, or you can buy them dried online. They are used like bay leaves to impart a unique and delicious flavor unlike any other spice I've tried!

Recommended with: Brown basmati rice, chickpeas, cooked carrots, and green beans, topped with chopped cilantro.

Ginger Miso Sauce

This quick and easy sauce is one of my go-to recipes for dressing up a bowl of grains and veggies with tamari almonds, so tangy and delicious!

MAKES 2 CUPS

½ cup water, more as needed
¼ cup raw cashews
¼ cup tamari
¼ cup tahini
⅓ cup apple cider vinegar
Juice of 1 lemon
2" fresh ginger
2 small shallots
3 Tbsp light miso

Add all ingredients to a high-speed blender, and blend several minutes until completely smooth.

Recommended with: Chopped and steamed kale, raw chopped purple cabbage, cubes of cooked butternut squash, quinoa, tamari almonds (see **Odds and Ends**), topped with fresh chopped mint leaves.

Curry Your Flavor Sauce

Blurring the lines between a sauce and a dressing, this sauce is fast and light, sweet and tangy.

MAKES 2 CUPS

½ cup water
½ cup raw cashews
½ cup water
⅓ cup apple cider vinegar
½" fresh ginger
2 cloves garlic
2 Tbsp white miso
2 Medjool dates
1 tsp Madras Curry Powder (see **Odds and Ends**)

Add all ingredients to a high-speed blender and blend until smooth.

Recommended with: Quinoa, roasted corn, shredded carrots, steamed kale, sundried tomatoes, extra-firm tofu cut into ½" cubes, topped with sesame seeds.

Golden Cheezy Sauce

This recipe was one of the first all-purpose sauces I used that makes everything taste good; my boys always ask for seconds with this sauce!

MAKES 4½ CUPS

3½ cups water
½ cup raw cashews
½ cup all-purpose flour
2 Tbsp tamari
1½ tsp garlic powder
1 tsp onion powder
1 tsp sea salt
½ tsp turmeric powder
1 cup nutritional yeast

Add water and cashews to a high-speed blender and blend until smooth, about 2 minutes. Add the remaining ingredients and blend further until the sauce is smooth.

Pour the sauce into a medium saucepan and cook on medium heat, using a whisk to stir constantly until the sauce thickens, about 5 minutes.

Note: Instead of taking the extra time to combine flour and margarine first to make roux, this recipe lets you skip that step and cut out the margarine completely. Instead of all-purpose flour, you can use chickpea flour or other alternatives to make this recipe gluten-free.

Recommended with: My favorite meal with the Golden Cheezy Sauce is brown basmati rice and steamed broccoli sprinkled with chopped pecans and paprika.

Rich and Delicious Mushroom Gravy

Don't save this recipe just for the holidays; this is a quick, delicious sauce to use whenever you want a hearty bowl meal!

MAKES 4½ CUPS

1 medium white onion, chopped
2 cups fresh button mushrooms, chopped
4 cloves garlic, chopped
3 cups vegetable broth
¼ cup dry red wine
¼ cup whole-wheat flour
3 Tbsp nutritional yeast
2 Tbsp thyme
2 Tbsp rosemary
2 Tbsp tamari
1 tsp sea salt
1 tsp sage
¼ tsp ground black pepper

Water-sauté the onions, mushrooms, and garlic in a medium saucepan until the onions are translucent. Add the remaining ingredients to a high-speed blender and puree until smooth, then pour into the saucepan with the onions, mushrooms, and garlic. Cook the gravy over medium heat and whisk often until the gravy has thickened to the correct consistency; if you prefer the consistency to be thicker, whisk in more flour.

Note: As with the Golden Cheezy Sauce, which also uses flour, instead of taking the extra time to combine flour and margarine first to make roux, this recipe lets you skip that step and cut out the margarine completely. Instead of all-purpose flour, you can use chickpea flour or other alternatives to make this recipe gluten-free.

Recommended with: Chickpeas, mashed or cubed potatoes, green beans.

Creole Remoulade Sauce

With this sauce, we travel to New Orleans for a combination of French and Southern US cuisine, often used as a condiment, but we'll use the same flavors to make a delicious Creole sauce!

MAKES 2 CUPS

½ box Mori-Nu silken tofu
½ cup raw cashews
¼ cup water
2 cloves garlic, peeled
Juice of ½ lemon
3 scallions, diced
2 Tbsp chopped parsley
2 Tbsp Dijon mustard
1 tsp smoked paprika
1 tsp sriracha
1 tsp tamari
1 tsp dried oregano
1 tsp dried basil
1 tsp sea salt
½ tsp dried thyme
½ tsp ground black pepper

Blend the tofu, cashews, water, garlic, and lemon juice in a high-speed blender until smooth. Add to a 1-quart Mason jar, then add the remaining ingredients and shake well until combined.

Recommended with: Long-grain brown rice, diced tomatoes, sautéed green bell pepper, yellow onion, diced celery, Vegan Ground "Meat" Crumbles (see **Odds and Ends**) but cut the sausages instead of using the food processor to crumble them.

Nutmeg Stroganoff Sauce

This sauce is a great pairing with my Swedish-Style Vegan Meat-balls. Pasta with stroganoff sauce was one of my favorite meals as a kid, and I was delighted to make a healthy, whole-food version for my family to enjoy.

MAKES 4½ CUPS

½ cup raw cashews
3 cups water
3 Tbsp all-purpose flour
½ medium carrot, unpeeled
½ stalk celery
¼ medium yellow onion
1 Tbsp tamari
1 tsp apple cider vinegar
1 tsp Dijon mustard
1 tsp sea salt
½ tsp ground black pepper
½ tsp ground nutmeg
1 bay leaf

Blend all ingredients together in a high-speed blender except for the bay leaf, and pour into a medium saucepan and simmer with the bay leaf for 10 minutes. Whisk until the sauce has thickened. Remove the bay leaf and serve.

Recommended with: Brown rice and quinoa fusilli pasta, Swed-ish-Style Vegan Meatballs (see **Burgers and Balls**), steamed kale, sautéed mushrooms, and onions.

Carolina Gold BBQ Sauce

Carolina Gold BBQ Sauce is the mustardy, sweet-and-tangy version of traditional barbeque sauces you normally find in stores. You can use this as a sauce for bowl meals in addition to using it as a dipping sauce; it tastes so good, you won't want to limit it to being just a condiment!

MAKES 2¼ CUPS

½ cup yellow mustard
¼ cup tamari
¼ cup apple cider vinegar
¼ cup raw cashews
1 fresh medium tomato
8 Medjool dates
3 cloves garlic
1 Tbsp blackstrap molasses
1½ tsp ground black pepper
¼ tsp liquid smoke
¼ cup water

Blend all ingredients together, the simmer in a medium saucepan for 15 minutes.

Recommended with: Russet baked potato wedges, kebab skewers with cubes of tofu, onion, red bell pepper.

A Different Kind of Dashi Sauce

Dashi is a broth made from soaking dried shiitake mushrooms, but in this recipe we'll change course a bit and make a healthy and delicious sauce that I love to pour over a bowl meal of sushi ingredients. I love vegetable nori rolls, but sometimes it's easier just to put all the fillings together as a bowl and enjoy the delicious taste without having to roll and slice, over and over. This healthy sauce is just the thing to take a sushi bowl to the next level.

MAKES 3 CUPS

1" strip of dried kombu
1 cup dried shiitake mushrooms
2 cup hot water
6 Medjool dates
½ cup tamari
2 Tbsp apple cider vinegar
1 tsp powdered ginger, or 1" fresh
¼ tsp wasabi paste

Soak the kombu and shiitake mushrooms in hot water for 10 minutes, then add to a high-speed blender with the remaining ingredients, and puree until smooth. Pour into a small saucepan and simmer for 5 minutes, stirring regularly.

Recommended with: Short-grain brown rice, cooked carrots, cubes of avocado, chopped cucumber, cubed tofu, and shredded sheets of nori, sprinkled with sesame seeds.

Colonel's Herbs and Spices Sauce

While few people know the Colonel's secret blend of herbs and spices, one can certainly guess! Pour this savory sauce over a hearty bowl of healthy ingredients, and our feathered friends will thank you for it!

MAKES 4½ CUPS

3 cups water
1 cup raw cashews
1 clove garlic
¼ of a medium yellow onion
¼" fresh ginger
3 Medjool dates
3 tsp smoked paprika
1 tsp cayenne pepper
1 tsp dried sage
1 tsp dried oregano
1 tsp dried basil
1 tsp dried marjoram
1 tsp ground coriander
1 tsp ground black pepper
1 tsp sea salt
½ tsp ground allspice

Add the first six ingredients to a high-speed blender and blend until smooth. In a 1-quart Mason jar, add all the spices, then pour in the blender mixture, cover the jar, and shake well.

Note: Since it takes some time to measure out all the dry ingredients, if you make this sauce regularly you can save time by combining all the spices in larger quantities and storing in a covered container. Then you can spoon it out as needed (the spices to make one batch of this sauce fills ¼ cup total).

Recommended with: Cooked red potato cubes, cooked carrots and kale, tofu cubes, topped with chopped chives.

Polish-Style Herb Sauce

Many countries have unique blends of spices and herb that are not necessarily well known outside of those cultures. A friend introduced me to a store-bought seasoning mix used frequently in Polish cooking, and it was delicious, but I couldn't pronounce half of the additives and artificial flavors, so I decided to recreate the flavors using fresh, whole-food ingredients, without the MSG. I think I got pretty close, and this sauce tastes delicious over potatoes, Polish-style Sausage, and hearty vegetables.

MAKES 3 CUPS

1 medium carrot
1 parsnip
1 cup water
½ cup raw cashews
1 stalk celery
½ medium yellow onion
½ tsp turmeric powder
¼ cup nutritional yeast
1 tsp sea salt
1 clove garlic
¼ cup finely chopped parsley

Cook the carrot and parsnip in the cup of water until soft, then add the mixture to a high-speed blender with the cashews. Add the remaining ingredients except for the parsley and blend. Once completely pureed, pour into a 1-quart Mason jar with the chopped parsley and shake well.

Recommended with: Buckwheat or boiled potatoes, cooked carrots, golden beets, chopped green cabbage, sliced Polish-Style Vegan Sausage (see **Odds and Ends**).

Thai Peanut Sauce

This sauce is a favorite mixed into noodle bowls or as a dipping sauce for chopped veggies and crispy tofu cubes.

MAKES 2½ CUPS

1 cup roasted peanuts, unsalted
1 cup water
½ cup tamari
2 Tbsp toasted sesame oil
2 Medjool dates
3 cloves garlic
1" fresh ginger
1 tsp sriracha
Juice of 1 lime

Combine all ingredients in a high-speed blender, and blend for several minutes until completely smooth.

Recommended with: Stir-fry rice noodles or linguini, Sesame Tofu Cubes (see **Odds and Ends**), frozen stir-fry vegetables, topped with chopped scallions.

Garlic Chipotle Aioli Sauce

Normally, I'd say using store-bought vegan mayo as the base of sauce would be a little extra indulgent with all the fat, but swapping the cashews for oil dramatically reduces the fat and makes a creamy, rich garlicky sauce that's a delightful addition to any bowl meal.

MAKES 3 CUPS

½ cup raw cashews
1 cup water
1 box of Mori-Nu 12 oz. box silken tofu
3 cloves garlic
Juice of 1 lemon
2 tsp chipotle chili powder
1 ½ tsp sea salt
¼ tsp liquid smoke
¼ cup chopped chives

Add all ingredients to a high-speed blender except for the chives, and blend until smooth. Mince the chives and stir into the sauce.

Recommended with: Long-grain brown rice, Vegan Ground "Meat" Crumbles (see **Odds and Ends**), stir-fried corn, yellow onion, green bell pepper, topped with chopped cilantro.

Thai Green Curry Sauce

Traditionally in Thai restaurants, green curry is served as more of a broth than a sauce. If you want this sauce to be similar to a broth, just add some water to the saucepan. The cheater's way to make Thai curries is to buy curry paste in a can and add a few teaspoons to coconut milk, but it's not much harder to make it from scratch, plus you can control the ingredient amounts to add more or less of the flavors you want (like hot peppers!).

MAKES 3 CUPS

¼ cup coconut manna
2 cups water
2 Medjool dates
½–1 Jalapeno pepper, deseeded
3 cloves garlic, peeled
½ stalk lemongrass (2" long, ¼' round)
1 shallot
2" fresh ginger
2 kaffir lime leaves
Zest of 1 lime
1 Tbsp tamari
1 ½ tsp sea salt
½ tsp ground coriander
½ tsp ground cumin

Add all the ingredients to a high-speed blender, and blend until pureed. You can either simmer the sauce in a pan for 5–10 minutes, or add to a stir-fry pan with the recommended veggies and cook the sauce that way.

Note: Kaffir lime leaves can be found in Asian and natural markets in small jars; this is a specialty item that you may not use much but it's well worth seeking out (you can look online also), and it stores in the refrigerator for months.

Recommended with: Short-grain brown rice, extra-firm tofu, pressed and cubed, cubed zucchini, chopped bamboo shoots, chopped and steamed green bell pepper, chopped Thai eggplants or Japanese eggplant, string beans, topped with chopped fresh basil.

Perfectly Pesto Sauce

Pesto doesn't have to be an oily, unhealthy mess; let the fresh basil take center stage here. For anyone who thinks there's no such thing as too much basil, this recipe is for you!

MAKES 2 CUPS

½ cup pine nuts
½ cup raw walnuts
1½ cups fresh basil
1 red bell pepper
½ cup fresh cilantro
¼ cup nutritional yeast
Juice of 1 lemon
1 clove garlic
1 tsp sea salt

In a small skillet, toast the pine nuts and walnuts for several minutes, stirring continuously until they start to brown, then set aside. Add the remaining ingredients to a food processor and run until all ingredients are well combined.

Recommended with: Whole-wheat orzo, cannellini beans, roasted zucchini, cherry tomatoes, garlic, baby bella mushrooms.

Sun Dried Tomato Marinara Sauce

That store-bought marinara sauce in the jar is loaded with salt and sugar, and how long has it been sitting on the shelf? This sauce has lots of fresh tomato, garlic, and basil; nothing beats the taste of fresh marinara sauce!

MAKES 4½ CUPS

½ cup raw cashews
½ cup water
2 Medjool dates
3 medium tomatoes
1 cup finely chopped tomatoes
1 cup fresh basil
1 cup raw walnuts
1 cup sun-dried tomatoes, dry-packed not oil-packed
½ yellow onion
4 cloves garlic, peeled
1 ½ tsp sea salt
1 tsp dried oregano

Blend the cashews, water, dates, and 3 tomatoes in a high-speed blender until smooth, and set aside. Combine the remaining ingredients in a food processor, and blend until well combined, then add to a medium saucepan with the mix from the blender. Cook and stir on medium heat for 10 minutes.

Note: Here's a chance to try using spiralized zucchini instead of pasta, yet another way to add whole-food ingredients into your meal. There are expensive spiralizers on the market, but if you're spiralizer-curious, I had good luck with one of the inexpensive hand-held spiralizers that I picked up at a home goods store for ten dollars. Zucchini doesn't have a strong taste, and especially here with delicious sauce, sautéed veggies, and veggie meatballs, you may not even notice it's not pasta!

Recommended with: Spiralized zucchini noodles, sautéed mushrooms and spinach, Italian-Style Vegan Meatballs (see **Burgers and Balls**), Parmesan-Like Topping (see **Odds and Ends**).

Spinach and Artichoke Sauce

Spinach and artichokes pair well together in a dip, but also as a sauce for bowl meals. Here is a great example of loading up the sauce with healthy vegetables, sneaking in a few more servings of vegetables before you even get to the bowl meal itself!

MAKES 5 CUPS

2 cups frozen artichoke hearts, chopped
2 cups frozen spinach
½ cup raw cashews
1 cup water
1 medium tomato
1 tsp capers
3 cloves garlic
½ cup fresh basil, chopped
⅓ cup nutritional yeast
Juice of 1 lemon
1 Tbsp yellow mustard
2 tsp dried tarragon
1 tsp sea salt
½ tsp ground black pepper

Soak the frozen artichoke hearts and spinach in hot water in a mixing bowl for 10 minutes to thaw. Blend the cashews, water, tomato, capers, and garlic in a high-speed blender until smooth.

Drain the artichoke hearts and spinach, puree in a food processor and add both to a medium saucepan with the cashew/tomato sauce and the remaining ingredients. Cook over medium heat and stir occasionally for 10 minutes.

Recommended with: Small pasta shells, Vegan Italian-Style Sausage (see **Odds and Ends**), frozen Italian mixed vegetables (cauliflower, broccoli, zucchini, Italian green beans, red peppers, carrots, baby lima beans).

Super-Creamy Alfredo Sauce

This makes a great sauce for mac and cheese. It's also a nutritional powerhouse with both sweet potato and cauliflower. If you have cauliflower haters in your family, sneak it into this sauce and watch as they ask for seconds!

MAKES 4 CUPS

1 cup peeled and cubed sweet potato
½ head cauliflower, chopped
1½ cups water (saved from sweet potato and cauliflower)
½ cup raw cashews
⅓ cup nutritional yeast
3 cloves garlic, peeled
1 Tbsp prepared yellow mustard
1 tsp sea salt
½ tsp ground black pepper

Cook the sweet potato and cauliflower with enough water to cover on medium heat for 15 minutes.

Strain the water into another saucepan or metal bowl, and add the sweet potato and cauliflower to a blender with the remaining ingredients and blend until smooth.

Recommended with: Small shells or elbow pasta, air-fried tofu cubes covered with buffalo sauce and chopped, steamed kale.

Jamaican Jerk Sauce

Don't let the list of ingredients scare you away; this sauce is so great, it's well worth the effort! It has plenty of kick, but if you are more daring, you can add a Scotch Bonnet pepper.

MAKES 2½ CUPS

¼ cup raw cashews
¼ cup water
⅓ cup apple cider vinegar
2 Medjool dates
2 whole tomatoes
¼ cup blackstrap molasses
2 Tbsp tamari
1 bunch chopped scallions
2 cloves garlic
1" fresh ginger
1 tsp sea salt
½ tsp ground black pepper
1 tsp dried thyme
1 tsp smoked paprika
½ tsp ground chipotle pepper
½ tsp ground allspice
¼ tsp ground nutmeg
¼ tsp ground cinnamon

Add the cashews and water to a high-speed blender and blend for 1 minute, then add the remaining ingredients, and blend until completely smooth. Add to a saucepan and simmer over medium heat for 10 minutes, stirring frequently.

Note: This is a recipe you may want to make in large batches if you really like it, because it calls for a long list of ingredients. You can freeze this sauce in 1-pint Mason jars to use for later, fast and convenient!

Recommended with: This is a great utility sauce that works well over different combinations of beans, grains, and veggies, but if you want to mirror what you may find in a Jamaican restaurant, you can pour this sauce over long-grain brown rice, black beans, and cooked green cabbage seasoned with Jamaican curry powder.

Plant-Powered
Snacks

Healthy Snacks

Now it's time to address your burning question: *Where the hell are the desserts?* They're right here, in disguise. I love desserts, but when you are going for a whole-food, plant-based approach with no sugar or oil, the options for sweets go down dramatically. So, I compromise: I save the cake for restaurants, and what I make at my house is healthy and delicious without sugar and oil. A funny thing happens when you cut way back on sugar though: your sensitivity to sugar goes up and your craving for it goes down.

Are snacks really such an awful thing? Must we righteous-ly try to ignore our afternoon hunger pangs and try to hold out until dinner? Heck no—we'd be back into sacrificing territory! Maybe we're just going about snacking the wrong way. What if instead of breaking open the bag of chips and then trying to stop yourself from eating the whole bag, snacks could be like dessert but actually healthy?

Healthy Snacks as a System

You can make these healthy snacks in batches and keep them in the fridge or freezer, so when the snacking urge strikes, you'll have something yummy on hand. No processed foods necessary! I intentionally wrote these recipes to be rich and intense in flavor; a few of the Gingerbread Cookie Bites, for example, are delicious and satisfying, but you'll enjoy a few and stop there, instead of eating the whole bag.

Healthy Snacks

Chocolate Almond Bites

The almond pulp and vanilla extract gives these bites an almost cake-like consistency and taste.

MAKES 12 BITES

¾–1 cup of almond pulp (see Making Non-Dairy Milk in **Odds and Ends**)
1 cup Medjool dates (8 dates)
2 Tbsp almond butter
¼ Tsp sea salt
1 Tbsp vanilla extract
¼ cup chopped raw walnuts
¼ cup cacao nibs
Finely crushed roasted and salted peanuts

Blend almond pulp and dates together in a food processor for a minute, then add the almond butter, salt, and vanilla, and process until smooth. Add the walnuts and cacao nibs, and process further just until consistently mixed. Transfer the mixture to a bowl and start shaping the mixture into golf ball–sized balls. Next, roll the balls in different powder coatings as a finish, such as crushed peanuts.

Note: If you don't have a powerful food processor, soak the dates for several hours first.

Instead of almond pulp, you can grind almonds in a food processor just enough to make it a flour-like consistency (but if you process it too long it will start to become almond butter).

Double Chocolate Double Peanut Bites

I love the combination of chocolate and peanut butter, so why not double the fun?

MAKES 12 BITES

½ cup roasted peanuts, unsalted
½ ripe banana, mashed
¼ cup cacao powder
8 Medjool dates
2 Tbsp cacao nibs
4 squares graham cracker, crushed
¼ tsp espresso powder
¼ tsp sea salt
½ cup powdered peanut butter

Add the peanuts to a food processor and pulse, continuing to scrape down the sides until the peanuts have been broken down into small pieces. Add the banana, cacao powder, dates, cocoa nibs, crushed graham crackers, and sea salt, and continue to process for 1 minute. Roll the mixture into 1" balls. In a shallow bowl, roll each ball in powdered peanut butter. Refrigerate for 1 hour before serving.

Orange Chocolate Energy Bites

These bites are a favorite of my boys; they disappear fast in my house. Just don't tell them it's healthy!

MAKES 20 BITES

2 cups Medjool dates (approximately 16), pitted
1½ cups raw cashews
¾ cup raisins
¼ cup cacao powder
½ tsp orange extract
½ cup hemp seeds
Zest of 1 orange
¼ tsp espresso powder

Using a food processor, blend all ingredients until everything is combined and a thick paste forms, which may take several minutes. Roll the paste into ball form, and refrigerate 30 minutes before serving.

Dark Chocolate Cherry Energy Bites

Like my Black Forest Smoothie, this recipe celebrates the magical combination of chocolate and cherries!

MAKES 16 BITES

½ cup raw almonds
½ cup raw cashews
½ cup raw pumpkin seeds
½ cup finely shredded coconut
⅓ cup raw cacao powder
½ cup quick oats
4 Medjool dates
2 Tbsp maple syrup
1 tsp almond extract
¼ tsp espresso powder
¼ tsp vanilla extract
⅛ tsp sea salt
½ cup fresh or dried cherries
½ cup finely shredded coconut

Combine all ingredients except coconut in a food processor, and blend until the mixture is well combined. Scoop 1 Tbsp of the mixture and roll between your palms into a ball. Add the shredded coconut to a plate and roll each ball through the coconut to coat the ball, applying enough pressure to embed the shredded coconut into the ball. Refrigerate for 30 minutes, then serve or transfer to a plastic bag and store in the refrigerator or freezer.

Piña Colada Energy Bites

These tropical treats are a breeze to make and delight the senses!

MAKES 12 BITES

⅔ cup large coconut flakes
½ cup dried pineapple chunks
4 Medjool dates
½ cup raw walnuts
¼ cup frozen pineapple, thawed
4 squares graham cracker
2 Tbsp coconut manna
¼ tsp sea salt
½ cup finely shredded coconut

Combine all ingredients except the coconut in a food processor, and pulse until well blended. Form the mixture into 1" balls and then roll them in shredded coconut. Refrigerate for 1 hour before serving.

Gingerbread Cookie Bites

Gingerbread cookie recipes typically call for eggs, brown sugar, a lot of butter, and processed white flour, but it's the spices that make them taste the way they do, not all that junk!

MAKES 12 BITES

1 cup quick oats
8 Medjool dates
½ cup cooked sweet potato
5 squares graham cracker
2 Tbsp hemp seeds
1" fresh ginger
1 Tbsp blackstrap molasses
1 tsp Nutiva Buttery Coconut Spread
1 tsp ground cinnamon
1 tsp vanilla extract
½ tsp ground nutmeg
¼ tsp sea salt
⅛ tsp ground cloves

Add ingredients to a food processor and pulse until the mixture is well combined.

Roll into 1" balls and refrigerate for 1 hour before serving.

Chocolate Chili Energy Bites

By now you may have noticed I have a thing for chocolate. . . . In this recipe, we spice things up—not too much, just enough to give these bites a kick!

MAKES 20 BITES

1 cup raw walnuts
½ cup frozen mango chunks, thawed
½ cup quick oats
¼ cup cacao powder
¼ cup goji berries
6 Medjool dates
2 Tbsp cacao nibs
½ tsp chipotle powder
¼ tsp espresso powder
¼ tsp sea salt

Add all the ingredients to a food processor, and blend several minutes until well combined.

Roll into 1" balls and refrigerate for 1 hour.

Coconut Mojito Energy Bites

This recipe is a class favorite—people are amazed at how something so delicious can be so healthy. The combination of fresh mint, lime, and coconut make these treats disappear quickly!

MAKES 12 BITES

½ cup large coconut flakes, or ⅛ of a fresh coconut
½ cup raw cashews
8 Medjool dates
¼ cup fresh mint leaves
Zest of 1 lime
Juice of ½ lime
2 Tbsp coconut manna
¼ tsp sea salt
¼ tsp mint extract
½ cup finely shredded coconut

Add all the ingredients except the coconut to a food processor and pulse until the mixture is well combined.

Roll the mixture into 1" balls. Pour finely shredded coconut into a bowl and roll each ball in the coconut to coat, then refrigerate for 1 hour.

Pumpkin Spice Energy Bites

As fall rolls in, I like to keep these bites in the freezer for when the pumpkin spice urge strikes!

MAKES 15 BITES

1 cup quick oats
8 Medjool dates
½ cup cooked or canned pumpkin puree
⅓ cup pepitas
4 squares graham cracker
2 Tbsp hemp seeds
2 tsp ground cinnamon
1 tsp Nutiva Buttery Coconut Spread
1 tsp vanilla extract
½ tsp powdered ginger
½ tsp ground nutmeg
½ tsp sea salt
⅛ tsp ground allspice
⅛ tsp ground cloves
Toasted coconut shreds

Add all the ingredients except the coconut to a food processor and pulse until the mixture is well combined.

Roll into 1" balls, coat with toasted coconut shreds, and refrigerate for 1 hour before serving.

The Seed of Power Bars

Because all that vegans eat are nuts and seeds, right? These bars are a boost of power when you need it, sweet and tasty and loaded with nutrition!

MAKES 5 BARS

1 cup frozen mango chunks, thawed
1 cup Medjool dates
½ cup raisins
1 cup shredded coconut
½ cup raw walnuts
½ cup pumpkin seeds (pepitas)
½ cup sunflower seeds
¼ cup sesame seeds
¼ cup hemp seeds
¼ cup cacao powder
2 Tbsp cacao nibs
¼ tsp sea salt

Combine the mango, dates, and raisins in a food processor and pulse until well combined, scraping down the sides as needed. Add the remaining ingredients to the food processor and continue to blend for 1 minute.

Pour the mixture into an 8" x 8" brownie pan lined with parchment paper, and use a spatula to pat down the mixture, pressing it into the pan evenly. Bake for 20 minutes at 325° F, then remove from the pan and cool on a baking rack.

Cut into 2" x 6" bars, and keep refrigerated in a resealable bag.

Oatmeal Raisin Bars

These bars are a flashback to the tastes of my childhood, updated with whole-food, unprocessed ingredients for a healthier spin!

MAKES 5 BARS

1 banana, mashed
1 cup quick oats
8 Medjool dates
2 Tbsp hemp seeds
2 Tbsp almond butter
1 Tbsp blackstrap molasses
1 tsp ground cinnamon
½ tsp sea salt
½ cup raisins

Add all the ingredients except the raisins to a food processor, and pulse until the mixture is well combined.

Scoop the mixture into a mixing bowl and stir in the raisins. Pour the mixture into a loaf pan lined with parchment paper along the bottom and up the sides, and bake for 20 minutes at 325° F. Pull on the sides of the parchment paper to lift the cooked loaf out of the pan and onto a cooling rack. Once the loaf is cooled, cut into squares and store in the refrigerator.

Turkish Delightful Bars

Rosewater gives these bars a unique, flowery fragrance. They are delightful for your taste buds and your health!

MAKES 5 BARS

1 cup Turkish figs
½ cup fresh (or frozen and thawed) strawberries
½ cup quick oats
½ cup raw pistachios
4 Medjool dates
2 tsp rosewater
½ tsp ground cardamom
¼ tsp sea salt

Add all ingredients to a food processor and blend until well combined. Line a loaf pan with parchment paper and press the mixture into the pan. Bake for 20 minutes at 325° F. Once the pan has cooled, slice into bars and keep refrigerated until serving.

Maple Walnut Ice Cream

Frozen fruit ice cream is a quick and healthy alternative to store-bought ice cream or using an ice cream maker. While this recipe is for maple walnut-flavored, you can use different frozen fruit combinations with extracts and flavorings; there are plenty of ideas just in the Breakfast Smoothies chapter to start with. It's best to make frozen fruit ice cream and serve it immediately; if you store this in the freezer it will get solid, and I think it's better as a soft-serve consistency. Because there is not much fat in the recipe, it won't get creamy if frozen like ice cream.

MAKES 1½ CUPS

2 frozen bananas
½ cup raw walnuts
1 Tbsp maple syrup
1 tsp vanilla extract
Several dashes ground cinnamon

In a food processor, puree the frozen bananas until soft, stopping to scrape down the sides several times as needed. Add the remaining ingredients and process for another 30 seconds.

Chocolate Mousse Cups

*This is the recipe I make for people who say they hate tofu! So choc-
olatey and rich, nobody's going to notice or care that there is tofu in
this. I make this recipe in individual mousse cups but you can make it
as a pie instead; this makes it easier to bring to parties to share with
family and friends . . . if you feel like sharing.*

MAKES 12 MOUSSE CUPS

FOR THE CRUST:
¾ cup raw pecans
1 cup dates
Pinch of salt
1 tsp pure vanilla powder
3 Tbsp cacao powder

FOR THE MOUSSE:
1½ cups soft silken tofu
¼ tsp espresso powder
2 Tbsp maple syrup or agave
2 bars of high-quality chocolate, 80–90% cacao

Add the crust ingredients to a food processor, and blend until well
combined. Press the mixture into the bottom of a mini-cheesecake pan or mini-tart pan; there should be enough for 12 mousse
cups. Place the pan in the refrigerator to cool while you make the
mousse.

Add the tofu, espresso powder, and maple syrup to a food
processor or high-powered blender. Use a knife or hand chopper
to chop the chocolate bars into small pieces, and melt the chocolate in a double-boiler pan or in the microwave, heating until

mostly melted and stirring for the remainder, as the heat of the melted chocolate will melt the remaining chocolate. You want to avoid heating the chocolate too much so it doesn't solidify again. Pour the melted chocolate into the food processor or blender, and process until the tofu and chocolate are mixed well. Pour the mixture into the mini-cheesecake pan (approximately 2 Tbsp per mousse cup), and use the back of a spoon to smooth the top of each, then dust the pan with cacao powder. Place the pan in the refrigerator and chill for several hours before serving.

Peppermint Blizzard Rolls

People have told me they would buy this cookbook for this recipe alone!
These blizzard rolls take some time to prepare, but you'll get paid in
smiles and oohs and ahhs in return!

MAKES 10 PIECES

FOR THE ROLLS:
12 Medjool dates
⅓ cup quick oats
⅓ cup raw pecans
3 Tbsp cacao powder
Half a 75% cacao chocolate bar (I prefer using mint chocolate
for an extra mint flavor)
⅛ tsp sea salt

FOR THE FILLING:
⅔ cup finely shredded coconut
¼ cup coconut manna
¼ cup fresh mint
2 Tbsp agave nectar
1 tsp peppermint extract
¼ tsp salt

½ cup finely shredded coconut

In a food processor, add the ingredients for the roll and process
until well combined.

Tear off a square sheet of parchment paper and lay it across
a countertop or cutting board, and add the mixture. Flatten the
mixture into an 8" x 8" square using your hands, rolling pin, or a
food can until you have a thin, even base.

Rinse the bowl of the food processor, then add the filling ingredients and blend until well combined, scraping down the sides of the bowl as needed. Spread a line of the filling about 1" from the front edge of the roll. Slowly wrap the front edge of the roll over the filling, using the parchment paper for support, and continue to roll over the filling until the roll mixture is done. Spread a thin layer of shredded coconut on the parchment paper and pull the roll back through the coconut to coat the roll.

Refrigerate the roll for 1 hour, then slice the roll into 1" segments.

Vanilla Pudding

This recipe is a great example of how different the healthy, whole-food version can be from the instant-from-the-box recipe: this has a richer and deeper taste and is worth taking time to savor!

MAKES 2¼ CUPS

1½ cups soft silken tofu
6 Medjool dates
3 Tbsp raw cashews
1 tsp Nutiva Buttery Flavor Coconut Oil
2 tsp vanilla extract
¼ tsp sea salt
Pinch of vanilla powder

In a high-speed blender, blend all the ingredients except the vanilla powder until smooth, then spoon into individual serving bowls for pudding and sprinkle with vanilla powder. Refrigerate for 2 hours to chill before serving.

Deep Chocolate Pudding

Sweet potatoes are so healthy and nutritious, I'm always looking for new ways to sneak some in. Fortunately, you'll be too busy enjoying the chocolate pudding to notice!

MAKES 3 CUPS

1½ cups soft silken tofu
3 heaping Tbsp cacao powder
Half a bar 90% cacao chocolate, chopped and melted
8 Medjool dates
½ cup cooked sweet potato
3 Tbsp raw cashews
½ tsp espresso powder
¼ tsp sea salt

Combine all the ingredients in a high-speed blender, then pour into small bowls and chill before serving.

Healthy Tapioca Pudding from Scratch

Tapioca pudding has a bad reputation because of the glue-like consistency of instant tapioca, but if you rinse the tapioca pearls and leave out the eggs and all the sugar, this recipe could restore the faith of disbelievers!

MAKES 5 CUPS

3 cups water
½ cup tapioca pearls (large or small)
3 cups cashew milk (see **Odds and Ends**)
6 Medjool dates
¼ tsp sea salt
1 tsp Nutiva Buttery Flavor Coconut Oil
2 tsp vanilla extract
⅛ tsp ground nutmeg

Heat the water in a medium saucepan until it's almost boiling, then stir in the tapioca and turn heat to low. Stir occasionally and continue to cook for 15–20 minutes until the tapioca pearls become translucent. Pour through a metal mesh strainer and rinse the tapioca pearls; this will remove a lot of the starch from the tapioca that otherwise gives tapioca pudding the consistency of glue.

While the tapioca is cooking, add the cashew milk and dates to a high-speed blender and blend for several minutes until the dates are completely pureed.

In the saucepan, add the cashew milk and heat until it's almost boiling, then reduce to low heat and add the strained tapioca with the sea salt. Continue to cook and stir for another 5 minutes, then remove from heat, stir in the butter flavoring and vanilla, and pour the pudding into small bowls. Sprinkle with nutmeg and refrigerate until cool.

Note: Use a ratio of 1 cup cashews to 3 cups water for this recipe to make the pudding base thicker.

Lively Lemon Pudding

This lemon pudding is not for lightweights—if you like strong lemon, this recipe is for you!

MAKES 2½ CUPS

1½ cups soft silken tofu
Zest of ½ lemon
Juice of 1 lemon
6 Medjool dates
3 Tbsp raw cashews
2½ Tbsp agave nectar
½ tsp lemon extract
¼ tsp turmeric powder
¼ tsp sea salt

Add all the ingredients to a high-speed blender, and blend for 5 minutes until completely smooth. Pour into individual bowls and refrigerate for 2 hours to chill before serving.

Butterscotch Pudding

Butterscotch pudding was always a favorite of mine growing up, but can there be a healthy version? In this recipe, mild-tasting, healthy ingredients hide in the background leaving plenty of room for the butterscotch flavoring to take center stage!

MAKES 2½ CUPS

1½ cups soft silken tofu
½ cup cooked sweet potato
4 Medjool dates
3 Tbsp raw cashews
1 tsp Nutiva Buttery Flavor Coconut Oil
½ tsp vanilla extract
½ tsp sea salt
Several drops concentrated butterscotch flavoring

Add all ingredients to a high-speed blender and blend for several minutes until completely smooth; stopping to scrape down the sides as needed. Scoop into small bowls and chill several hours before serving.

Odds and Ends

Because where else am I going to put my recipe for Pickled Turnips? And don't say "in the trash." Even my boys will agree that in a falafel sandwich the pickled turnips are essential. This is the section for all the miscellaneous and misfit recipes that don't fit anywhere else.

Mediterranean Pickled Turnips

*This seems like the bastard recipe of this cookbook—nobody wants anything to do with it. So I'll make the sales pitch: you **need** this for falafel, whether for a wrap or as a dinner plate, it's a must-have. Some restaurants use pickles instead, but I say no way, this is what you have with falafel. I wouldn't be too excited to eat pickled turnips in almost any other context. This recipe lasts for months in the fridge, so I always have them ready for one of my favorite meals!*

MAKES 1 MASON JAR FULL OF DELICIOUSNESS

1½ large turnips
1 medium sized beet
1 bay leaf
1 cup apple cider vinegar
¼ cup coarse kosher salt or sea salt
1 Medjool date
½ Tbsp fennel seeds
1 large garlic clove, peeled
3 cups boiling water

Peel and wash turnips, cut into ½" strips and cut beet in the same way; add to a 1-quart Mason jar along with the bay leaf.

In a high-speed blender, mix the apple cider vinegar, salt, date, fennel seeds, and garlic with the boiling water, and blend for several minutes. Pour the marinade into the Mason jar until full and cover with the lid. Leave the jar on the counter for 4 days to ferment. Keep them in the fridge for up to 3 months.

Tamari Almonds

Tamari almonds make a great topping for bowl meals for an added boost of protein, or more dangerously, as a snack (a handful can quickly turn into several handfuls). You could buy them at the store, but they're so easy to make.

MAKES 2 CUPS

2 cups raw almonds
⅛ cup tamari

Preheat the oven to 300° F. Spread the almonds over a rimmed baking sheet, and bake in the oven for 10 minutes. Remove and stir, then bake for an additional 10 minutes.

Remove and pour into a metal mixing bowl, and shut the oven off. Stir in the tamari with the almonds, and continue to stir as the almonds absorb the tamari for several minutes.

Spread the almonds back onto the baking sheet, and return to the oven for at least another 10 minutes, letting the heat from the oven dry the almonds. Remove and store in a container for several weeks (if they don't get eaten first).

Bacony Vegan Bits

These crunchy Bacony Vegan Bits are a tasty topping for salads, bowl meals, and casseroles, plus they're an added boost of protein!

MAKES 1½ CUPS

One 8 oz. package of tempeh
2 Tbsp tamari
½ tsp liquid smoke

Preheat oven to 300° F. Add tempeh to a food processor, and pulse until chopped into granules, then spread onto a baking sheet and bake for 15 minutes.

Remove from the oven, pour into a metal mixing bowl, and add the liquid smoke. Stir well and return to the baking sheet and oven. Bake for an additional 10 minutes, then turn off the oven and keep the tempeh in the oven for another 15 minutes. Store in a covered container.

How to Make Coconut and Nut Butters

I started making my own nut butter because of the recipe for Chocolate Almond Bites. Raw almond butter from the health food store would cost 17 dollars, and it's not something I use a lot. I soon discovered that it's easy to make it at home if you have a good food processor. Making almond butter is essentially the same process as making other nut butters, and it's fairly easy to do, plus it will save you a lot of money. Unless you are buying fake peanut butter (a.k.a. "peanut-flavored spread," which is a disaster). This process also works well for making coconut butter / manna, which is harder to find at the store than coconut oil or coconut milk. Coconut butter / manna is the whole-food, unprocessed version that you can keep on hand without needing to use fresh coconuts.

It helps if you have a high-powered, large-capacity food processor, but a little one will do; I would expect a little food processor to get burned out after a while if you make nut butters regularly though. Add 1–2 cups of whatever nuts you want to use (raw or roasted, your preference) to the food processor fitted with the "S" blade, and run for about 5 minutes. Use a scraper to scrape down the sides to make sure all the nuts are getting processed, and run for several more minutes. Continue to stop, scrape down, and process until the nuts have been processed into nut butter. The nuts are chopped and heated by friction as they are processed, which softens the fat in the nuts and creams them so that they turn into nut butter. Raw almonds or coconut meat or dried shreds usually take about 10 minutes from start to finish, where softer nuts like cashews or peanuts will take less time.

This is an easy way to make different nut butters to use as spreads that aren't easy to find in stores, like pistachio or macadamia nut butter. There are lots of different flavor combinations out there for nut butters and additives like cinnamon or maple, so have fun experimenting!

There are other appliances that are able to do the same thing technically: the Vitamix is advertised as being able to make nut butters, and also there is a way to use a masticating juicer (like the Champion Juicer) to make nut butters, but this is one of the things that a good food processor is built to do over and over again, no sweat. When I make raw nut butter, I prefer to keep it in a container in the refrigerator, and I've found it to last a long time without going rancid.

How to Make Vegan Yogurt

I have to admit, I'm not a huge yogurt fan, but it does give just the right tang to smoothies like the Orange Creamsicle Smoothie, or to mango lassi, and occasionally I'll have need for it in different recipes. Sometimes on weekends I'll mix together a cup of fresh fruit, granola, and yogurt for a tasty treat. The vegan yogurt that I find in stores, if I can find it at all, is usually already flavored and sweetened, and it's expensive. This recipe makes plenty of plain yogurt and is much easier than the standard process of making yogurt with thermometers and fussy, expensive cultures. Unless it's something you want to make regularly and keep on-hand in the refrigerator, this is something you'll want to plan ahead for, as it takes a day from start to finish.

The key to this process is an electric pressure cooker; the Instant Pot Duo has a "yogurt" key that creates a sealed, temperature-consistent environment for the yogurt culture to grow in.

Making nondairy yogurt is the only instance in which I use store-bought nondairy milk instead of making my own; I recommend buying the shelf-stable boxed nondairy milk, unflavored and unsweetened (otherwise it will inhibit the culturing process). I prefer to use soymilk because it has a more neutral flavor than other nondairy milks, but you can use coconut, almond, or others as long as it doesn't have any additives, sweeteners, or flavoring.

The other ingredient I use to make yogurt is vegan acidophilus capsules; you can find these in different strengths in the supplement section of health food stores, usually refrigerated. I use the 10 billion CFU supplements and that does the trick for what I make.

In a quart Mason jar, pour a box of unflavored, unsweetened nondairy milk until it's almost full, then open three capsules of acidophilus and pour into the jar. Cover the jar and shake for a minute to mix the acidophilus with the nondairy milk, then pour the contents of the Mason jar into three pint Mason jars, and put all three jars into the Instant Pot (don't add lids to the jars). Put the lid of the Instant Pot in place, and turn the vent to the sealed position. Press the yogurt button, and increase the timer to 10 hours (I do this before I go to bed). When the timer goes off, add lids to the three jars, shake well, and place them in the refrigerator, leaving them for at least 12 hours. When you open the jars, the soy milk should be thickened and tangy, and you have your own nondairy vegan yogurt! If you want to thicken the yogurt further, pour it onto a layer of cheesecloth and suspend it over a bowl in the refrigerator for several hours, which will strain some of the water out.

This is a limited-utility yogurt; it works well for smoothies and in recipes, but on it's own? Well, it doesn't taste the same as the store-bought yogurt, so if that is what you're expecting, then this would take some getting used to. Add some fruit and try different flavors. It has all the probiotic health benefits of yogurt but without the fat, cholesterol, hormones, and everything else that comes with the dairy.

Eggless Mayo

Oh, mayonnaise, you're a magic ingredient making dressings and sauces rich and creamy, but you're anything but magical when it comes to my health. Mayonnaise is made from whipping egg yolks and vegetable oil, or the vegan version typically with just vegetable oil, but we can achieve the same creamy consistency with a small fraction of the fat by blending silken tofu and cashews!

MAKES 1¼ CUPS

Half a 12.5 oz. box Mori-Nu silken tofu
½ cup raw cashews
Juice of ¼ lemon
1 Tbsp apple cider vinegar
1 tsp dry mustard powder
½ tsp sea salt

In a high-speed blender, combine all ingredients until smooth. Store in the refrigerator for several days.

Oil-Free Savory Crust

I don't do a lot of baking, but for the times that I've needed a good savory crust I was dismayed by how much oil is called for to make the crust pliable. What would an oil-free crust be like? In this recipe, we swap out the oil for coconut manna for an oil-free, lower fat alternative.

MAKES 1 PIE CRUST

2 ½ cups whole wheat pastry flour
1 ½ tsp onion powder
1 tsp sea salt
½ cup + 2 Tbsp water
¾ cup coconut manna / butter

Mix together the dry ingredients first, then add the water and coconut manna and mix by hand for 5 minutes, adding flour if necessary if it's sticking to your hands. Place the dough ball in the refrigerator for 5 minutes to cool before using, or wrap and freeze the dough for later use. For pre-baked circles or squares, roll out on a floured surface, place on a baking sheet covered with parchment paper, and bake at 425° F for 7 minutes.

Sesame Tofu Cubes

I've made these seasoned and crispy tofu cubes for people in my Using an Air Fryer 101 class who had no love for tofu, and they ate them right up!

MAKES 2 CUPS

One 15 oz. block of extra-firm tofu
2 Tbsp nutritional yeast
2 tsp toasted sesame oil
3 Tbsp tamari
1 tsp maple syrup
1 Tbsp sesame seeds

Drain and press the tofu for 15 minutes. Use paper towels to absorb more of the water from the tofu, then cut the tofu into ½" cubes.

Add the nutritional yeast, sesame oil, and tamari to a large mixing bowl and mix together, then add the tofu cubes to coat. In a large frying pan, fry the tofu cubes, regularly turning with a metal spatula until all sides are crispy. Return the tofu cubes to the mixing bowl and toss with the maple syrup and sesame seeds.

Note: If you want to use an air fryer for the tofu, cook at 370° F for 10 minutes, remove, and shake in the basked, then cook for an additional 8 minutes.

Sambar Powder

I prefer the taste of homemade spice blends to what I find in stores, and this way I can control the ingredients I use and their quantities (Sambar blends usually include an almost inhuman amount of dried red chilies, which is more than this mere mortal can handle). Some of the ingredients in this recipe you'll need to find either at an Indian market or order online, which you can purchase in small quantities.

MAKES ⅔ CUP

6 Tbsp coriander seeds
15 curry leaves
3 Tbsp chana dal
1 Tbsp cumin seeds
1 Tbsp dried red chili powder
1 Tbsp whole black peppercorns
1 tsp fenugreek seeds
1 tsp mustard seeds
1 tsp turmeric powder

Add the whole spices to a spice grinder, coffee grinder, food processor with an "S" blade, or dry blender container, and process until the spices are ground to a powder. Add the ground spices to a small cast-iron skillet and heat the spices on medium-low for several minutes, stirring constantly, until they become aromatic and toasted. Let the mixture cool, then pour through a fine strainer or sifter into a spice jar. Cover and keep up to several months in your pantry.

How to Make Vegan Sausages

If you're thinking, *Gross, vegan sausages; what do you even put in that?*, have you ever taken a look or thought about what goes into making meat sausages? Seriously, it's literally one step above what goes into cat food. The thing is, with all the disgusting slaughterhouse byproducts that go into meat sausages, they have to add a heap of salt and spices to get it to be edible, so when you like the taste of sausages, it's really the salt and spices you enjoy. Why not add that to natural ingredients that aren't the equivalent of cat food? I don't generally use a lot of wheat gluten / seitan because it is a step away from a whole-food diet, but there are times I like to include vegan sausages: on the grill in the summer, mixed in with pasta sauce, or sliced on top of bowl meals as a protein. You can find different vegan sausages in stores, but they're easy enough to make and store for later, plus these recipes are less processed.

One note before we get to the recipes: these vegan sausages don't taste exactly like meat sausages. These vegan sausages are their own thing. They're like cousins instead of identical twins—in the same family and fun to hang out with. So expectation is everything here; if you make these expecting them to be exactly the same in taste and texture as meat sausages, you'll be disappointed. Enjoy them for what they are (healthier and similar taste but without any animals having to die) instead of what they aren't (exactly like meat).

Italian-Style Vegan Sausages

I like to keep these vegan sausages on-hand as a quick addition to stir-fries or marinara sauce for Italian dishes!

MAKES 6 SAUSAGES

Half a 15 oz. block extra-firm tofu
½ cup nutritional yeast
2 Tbsp onion powder
1 Tbsp fennel seeds
2 tsp ground black pepper
2 tsp smoked paprika
2 tsp smoked sea salt
1 tsp dried oregano
6 cloves garlic, peeled
2 Tbsp tamari
½ cup white wine
6 soaked sundried tomatoes, chopped
½ cup fresh basil
1 cup vital wheat gluten

Drain and press the tofu for at least 15 minutes.

Combine the dry ingredients in a food processor with an "S" blade, and process for 1 minute. Add the garlic, tamari, white wine, tomatoes, and basil, and process for several minutes until well combined. Transfer to a large mixing bowl, then add the wheat gluten. Mix with your hands until all ingredients are combined.

Divide the mixture into six equal parts, and form each part into a long sausage shape. Wrap each sausage in tinfoil, and twist the ends (as the sausage cooks, the foil with give it a firm shape). Add each wrapped sausage to a steamer and cook for 45 minutes, then put them in the refrigerator for several hours for them to firm up more. At this point they are ready to serve, or you can store them in the refrigerator for several days, or store them in the freezer in a plastic freezer bag (unwrap them from the foil before freezing).

Polish-Style Vegan Sausages

After much research into how kielbasa is made (trust me, you don't want to know; I'm still trying to understand how the active ingredient in gunpowder can be considered a safe food additive), I learned what seasonings to use to make my own vegan version. Kielbasa it isn't, but it is a tasty, savory sausage to enjoy in stir-fries and bowl meals.

MAKES 6 SAUSAGES

Half a 15oz. block extra-firm tofu
2 Tbsp beet root powder
1 Tbsp marjoram
2 tsp smoked sea salt, or 2 tsp sea salt + ½ tsp liquid smoke
1 Tbsp ground black pepper
1 Tbsp caraway seeds
1 tsp mustard powder
½ tsp ground allspice
6 cloves garlic
½ cup white wine
1 cup vital wheat gluten

Drain the tofu and press for at least 15 minutes.

Combine the dry ingredients in a food processor with an "S" blade, and process for 1 minute. Add the garlic, wine, and tofu, and process for several minutes until well combined. Empty the ingredients into a large mixing bowl, then add the wheat gluten. Mix with your hands until all ingredients are combined.

Divide the mixture into six equal parts, and form each part into a long sausage shape. Wrap each sausage in tinfoil, and twist the ends (as the sausage cooks, the foil with give it a firm shape). Add each wrapped sausage to a steamer and cook for 45 minutes, then put them in the refrigerator for several hours for them to firm up more. At this point they are ready to serve, or you can store them in the refrigerator for several days, or store them in the freezer in a plastic freezer bag (unwrap them from the foil before freezing).

Vegan Breakfast Sausage Patties

When the weekend hits and I'm in the mood for a full breakfast, I love a side of these savory breakfast sausage patties—a much healthier and less processed version to start the day with than what you'd find at the supermarket!

MAKES 12 PATTIES

1 Tbsp dried sage
2 tsp smoked sea salt (or 2 tsp sea salt and ½ tsp liquid smoke)
½ tsp thyme
½ tsp fennel seeds
½ tsp ground black pepper
½ tsp dried mustard
¼ tsp ground nutmeg
One 8 oz. Package of tempeh
1 medium tomato, chopped
1 medium shallot, chopped
1 tsp agave nectar
½ cup vital wheat gluten or chickpea flour
1 Tbsp canola oil (optional)

Combine the dry ingredients in a food processor with an "S" blade and process for 1 minute, then add the tempeh, tomato, shallot, and agave nectar, and process for several minutes until well combined.

Empty the ingredients into a large mixing bowl, then add the wheat gluten. Mix with your hands until all ingredients are combined. Roll the mixture into 1" balls, then flatten into patty shapes. Place all patties on a large plate and spray each side with cooking oil spray. I recommend cooking them in an air fryer for 8 minutes on 370° F—, then spraying both sides again and cooking them on the other side for an additional 8 minutes. Alternatively, you can spray the patties and cook them in the oven at 375° F in the same way, or fry them in a cast-iron skillet using a metal spatula.

Vegan Ground "Meat" Crumbles

Let's not talk about what's in ground beef. And the vegetarian "meat" crumbles at the supermarket are meatless but still have a long list of processed ingredients. In this recipe, I created a versatile vegan ground "meat" alternative that is much less processed but still full of flavor!

MAKES 2 CUPS

1 cup chopped shiitake mushrooms
4 cloves garlic, peeled
½ cup water
2 Tbsp tamari
2 Tbsp ketchup
2 tsp Better Than Bouillon, No Beef flavor
1 tsp onion powder
½ tsp smoked paprika
1 cup vital wheat gluten

Combine the mushrooms and garlic in the food processor fitted with an "S" blade, and pulse until well chopped. Transfer to a large mixing bowl, and add the remaining ingredients except the wheat gluten, and mix well. Add the wheat gluten and mix with your hands until the wheat gluten is completely mixed in.

Divide the mixture into five equal parts, and form each part into a long sausage shape. Wrap each sausage in tinfoil, and twist the ends (as the sausage cooks, the foil with give it a firm shape). Add each wrapped sausage to a steamer and cook for 45 minutes. Remove the foil and let cool, then chop roughly and add to the food processor, and pulse until the texture is similar to crumbles. This can be frozen and used as vegan ground meat as needed.

Note: Instead of crumbling the cooked sausages in a food processor, you can keep the sausages whole and freeze them, then thaw and use as an all-purpose substitute for chunks of vegan beef in bowl meals or in soups.

Vegan Corned Beef

This is a variation of the Vegan Ground "Meat" Crumbles recipe (see **Odds and Ends***); in this case we're adding pickling spices to mimic the flavor of brined corned beef.*

MAKES 2 CUPS

1 cup chopped shiitake mushrooms
4 cloves garlic
½ cup water
2 Tbsp tamari
2 Tbsp ketchup
1 Tbsp agave nectar
2 tsp Better Than Bouillon, No Beef flavor
1 tsp onion powder
½ tsp smoked paprika
¼ tsp ground allspice
¼ tsp ground coriander
¼ tsp ground cloves
¼ tsp ground mustard seed
⅛ tsp ground cardamom
⅛ tsp powdered ginger
⅛ tsp ground cinnamon
1 tsp sea salt
1 cup vital wheat gluten

Combine the mushrooms and garlic in the food processor fitted with an "S" blade, and pulse until it's well chopped. In a large mixing bowl, combine the mushrooms with the remaining ingredients, including the pickling spices, except the wheat gluten, and mix well. Add the wheat gluten and mix with your hands until the wheat gluten is completely mixed in. Divide the mixture into six equal parts, and form each part into a long sausage shape. Wrap each sausage in tinfoil, and twist the ends (as the sausage cooks, the foil with give it a firm shape). Add each wrapped sausage to a steamer and cook for 45 minutes. Remove the foil and let cool, then chop roughly and add to the food processor, and pulse until the texture is similar to crumbles. This can be frozen and used as vegan ground meat as needed.

Unholy Swiss Cheese Sauce

*This recipe isn't in the **Bowls and Sauces** chapter because this sauce is best used as a condiment for veggie burgers. It's very tangy due to the miso, nutritional yeast, and the lemon juice, so it's too strong to use as a sauce for bowl meals, but as a sauce to spread over veggie burgers it hits the spot!*

MAKES 2 CUPS

1 cup raw cashews
1 cup water
⅓ cup white miso
½ cup nutritional yeast
Juice of 1 lemon
1 tsp sea salt

Blend all the ingredients together in a high-speed blender until completely smooth.

Ethiopian Berbere Spice Mix

There is a limit to how much heat my palate can take, and, generally speaking, Berbere spice recipes are beyond what I can handle, admittedly. I love the rich mixture of spices though, so I've toned down the heat some in order to let the rest of the spice flavors shine through, one of the things that makes Ethiopian food taste so great to me! You can buy Berbere spice in some natural and ethnic markets, but making your own lets you control what goes in, and taking the time to make this yourself and keeping a bottle of it on hand for the times you'd want it is well worth it.

MAKES ¼ CUP

1 tsp ground coriander
1 tsp ground cardamom
1 tsp ground cumin
½ tsp ground fenugreek
½ tsp ground cinnamon
½ tsp ground nutmeg
¼ tsp ground cloves
2 tsp powdered ginger
2 tsp onion powder
2 tsp garlic powder
2 tsp ground chipotle
1 tsp sea salt (or black salt)
1 tsp ground black pepper
½ cup smoked paprika

If you have some of the first seven spices whole, use a small skillet to dry-roast them over medium heat for several minutes, stirring constantly. Next, use a spice grinder or high-speed blender to blend the mixture to a powder. In a small metal mixing bowl, add the roasted spices with the remaining ingredients and stir together, and store in a covered spice container.

Note: I prefer using smoked paprika and ground chipotle in this spice mix as I like the depth of flavor the smokiness adds, but you can use standard paprika and chili powder instead if you don't want the smoky flavor. Also, if you want your Berbere mix to be hotter, increase the amount of ground chipotle.

Lebanese 7-Spice Blend

Use this Lebanese spice mix to instantly lend a Middle-Eastern flavor to dishes!

MAKES ¼ CUP

1 Tbsp ground black pepper
1 Tbsp ground allspice
1 Tbsp ground cinnamon
1 tsp ground nutmeg
1 tsp ground coriander
1 tsp ground cloves
1 tsp powdered ginger

Combine all the ingredients together in a small mixing bowl, and store in an empty spice container.

Blasphemous Curry Powder

*I once attended an Indian cooking class where the instructor was asked if she, an Indian woman who made everything from scratch, used curry powder. Her horrified look said it all. "There is no such thing as curry powder; it is not a real thing. Forget that you have heard of that!" she said. There are many different spices used to make different curry dishes (**curry** is loosely translated to mean "sauce"), so the idea of there being one curry powder that represents what curry is supposed to taste like is sort of blasphemous. I love to cook Indian food, mostly from scratch, but there are some occasions when having a great spice combination premade for making quick meals is convenient (which probably makes me blasphemous), so here is the blend of spices I use for curry powder for you to use in such occasions (making you blasphemous as well). It tastes better than store-bought curry powder, and as long as you know that this spice blend is just one of many of the combinations you can use to make curry dishes, perhaps it's a little less blasphemous. . . .*

MAKES ⅓ CUP

2 Tbsp cumin seeds

2 Tbsp coriander seeds

1 Tbsp whole black peppercorns

2 tsp fenugreek seeds

1 tsp mustard seeds

1 tsp fennel seeds

¼ tsp whole cloves

10 curry leaves

2 tsp ground cinnamon

2 tsp ground cardamom

2 tsp turmeric powder

1 tsp ground nutmeg

1 tsp powered ginger

Add the whole spices to a spice grinder, coffee grinder, food processor with an "S" blade, or dry blender, and process until the spices are ground to a powder.

Add the ground spices and the remaining spices to a small cast-iron skillet and heat the spices on medium-low for several minutes, stirring constantly, until they become aromatic and toasted. Let it cool and pour through a fine strainer or sifter into a spice jar. Cover and keep this mixture up to several months in your pantry.

Note: The curry leaves *make* this spice blend, and this curry powder will last for months, so it's well worth the trouble of seeking these out. They're typically available at Indian markets but can also easily be ordered online. I recommend putting the rest of the curry leaves you don't use into a sealable plastic bag and keeping them in the freezer.

Sofrito

Sofrito is the base for a lot of Puerto Rican cooking. It's a fragrant mix of onion, garlic, peppers, and cilantro that isn't used as a sauce by itself but is added to many dishes while cooking to give it a punch of flavor. You may be able to find sofrito in the freezer section of the grocery store with other Hispanic foods, but there is a world of difference between homemade sofrito and store-bought, plus when you're cooking it, it smells amazing!

Full disclosure: This recipe is going to be a big pain in the neck if you follow it exactly, but it's worth the effort. Getting some of the ingredients for this recipe might be a scavenger hunt, and these are important ingredients, so you may really have to go the extra mile to acquire them. The good news is that sofrito does freeze well, and after I track down what I need from the Hispanic market, I make a big batch, pour the sofrito into ice cube trays, and freeze it. I store the cubes in a freezer bag and pull a few out as I need them, so that part is very convenient.

MAKES 4 CUPS

1 large yellow onion, roughly chopped
1 bunch fresh cilantro with stems, roots removed
1 bunch culantro with stems, roots removed, or substitute another
      bunch of cilantro
1 cup garlic cloves, peeled, or 1–2 bulbs of garlic
2 Cubanelle peppers (or substitute Anaheim peppers), deseeded
      and roughly chopped
1 red bell pepper, deseeded and roughly chopped
12 aji dulce peppers, deseeded and roughly chopped

Place the onion in a food processor and blend for 30 seconds first, then add the remaining ingredients and process until smooth, scraping down the sides as needed.

Note: You'll be most likely to find the culantro, Cubanelle peppers, and aji dulce peppers in Hispanic markets. Culantro is the cousin to cilantro, and it has long leaves. Cubanelle peppers look similar to Anaheim peppers, long and green. Aji dulce peppers look similar to habanero peppers but are not nearly as spicy, and they're usually green or red; this is a harder pepper to substitute for this recipe, so if you can't find any, then just omit instead of trying to substitute another pepper. The Cubanelle and Aji dulce peppers are not fiery peppers, so don't be afraid of them (but all the same, don't pull the seeds out and then rub your eyes).

Making Cold Teas

I like to have something on hand to drink in the fridge that is healthy and delicious, and these cold teas really hit the spot! These recipes make about 1 gallon of tea which I drink over the course of a week, but these can all be frozen in 1 quart Mason jars to drink later.

These recipes call for some dried flowers that are difficult to find in stores, so you can order them online and store them in your pantry. Cloth tea socks can also be ordered online; they fit over the mouth of a 1-gallon glass jar and can be washed and used many times.

Fresh Mint Tea

MAKES 12 CUPS

Add 10 cups water to a teakettle and heat until it's steaming/whistling. In the meantime, wash 1 cup of fresh mint and add to a high-speed blender with 2 cups water, blend slowly, then gradually increase speed and blend for several minutes until completely pureed. Pour through a tea sock fitted around the rim of a 1-gallon glass jar, then add the hot water from the teakettle. Leave the tea sock in place to let the mint steep for 1 hour, then remove the tea sock, and stir in ¼ cup maple syrup. Cover the jar, let cool, and then place overnight in the refrigerator. Stir before drinking.

Hibiscus Cold Tea

MAKES 12 CUPS

Add 10 cups water to a teakettle and heat until it's steaming/whistling. In the meantime, add ⅔ cup of dried hibiscus flowers to a high-speed blender with 2 cups tepid tap water, and let steep for 10 minutes. Run the blender for 2 minutes until completely pureed. Pour through a tea sock fitted around the rim of a 1-gallon glass jar, then add the hot water from the teakettle. Leave the tea sock in place to let steep for 1 hour, then remove the tea sock, and stir in ¼ cup maple syrup. Cover the jar, let cool, and then place overnight in the refrigerator. Stir before drinking.

Honeysuckle Flower and Honeydew Melon Tea
MAKES 12 CUPS
Add 10 cups water to a teakettle and heat until it's steaming/whistling. In the meantime, add ½ cup dried honeysuckle flowers and 1 cup of fresh honeydew melon to a high-speed blender with 2 cups tepid tap water, and let steep for 10 minutes. Run the blender for 2 minutes until completely pureed. Pour through a tea sock fitted around the rim of a 1-gallon glass jar, then add the hot water from the teakettle. Leave the tea sock in place to let steep for 1 hour, then remove the tea sock, and stir in ¼ cup maple syrup. Cover the jar, let cool, and then place overnight in the refrigerator. Stir before drinking.

Vanilla and Orange Blossom Tea
MAKES 12 CUPS
Add 10 cups water to a teakettle and heat until it's steaming/whistling. In the meantime, add 1 vanilla bean pod (or 3 tsp vanilla extract) and ⅔ cup of dried orange blossom flowers to a high-speed blender with 2 cups tepid tap water, and let steep for 10 minutes. Run the blender for 2 minutes until completely pureed. Pour through a tea sock fitted around the rim of a 1-gallon glass jar, and then add the hot water from the teakettle. Leave the tea sock in place to let steep for 1 hour, then remove the tea sock, and stir in ¼ cup maple syrup. Cover the jar, let cool, and place overnight in the refrigerator. Stir before drinking.

Jasmine Flower and Peach Tea

MAKES 12 CUPS

Add 10 cups water to a teakettle and heat until it's steaming or whistling. In the meantime, add ½ cup dried jasmine flowers and 1 cup fresh or frozen/thawed peaches to a high-speed blender with 2 cups tepid tap water, and let steep for 10 minutes. Run the blender for 2 minutes until completely pureed. Pour through a tea sock fitted around the rim of a 1-gallon glass jar, and then add the hot water from the teakettle. Leave the tea sock in place to let steep for 1 hour, then remove the tea sock, and stir in ¼ cup maple syrup. Cover the jar, let cool, and then place overnight in the refrigerator. Stir before drinking.

Osmanthus Flower and Darjeeling Oolong Tea

MAKES 12 CUPS

Add 10 cups water to a teakettle and heat until it's steaming/ whistling. In the meantime, add ½ cup dried osmanthus flowers and ¼ cup Darjeeling oolong tea to a high-speed blender with 2 cups tepid tap water, and let steep for 10 minutes. Run the blender for 2 minutes until completely pureed. Pour through a tea sock fitted around the rim of a 1-gallon glass jar, and then add the hot water from the teakettle. Leave the tea sock in place to let steep for 1 hour, then remove the tea sock, and stir in ¼ cup maple syrup. Cover the jar, let cool, and then place overnight in the refrigerator. Stir before drinking.

Juniper Berry and Orange Peel Tea

MAKES 10 CUPS

Add 10 cups water to a teakettle and heat until it's steaming/ whistling. In the meantime, add ½ cup dried juniper berries and ¼ cup dried orange peel to a tea sock fitted around the rim of a 1-gallon glass jar, and then add the hot water from the teakettle. Leave the tea sock in place to let the berries and orange peel steep for 1 hour, then remove the tea sock, and stir in ½ cup maple syrup. Cover the jar, let cool, and then place overnight in the refrigerator. Stir before drinking. Do not blend this tea in a blender like the other cold tea recipes.

Note: If you are trying to limit the amount of liquid sweetener you use, try substituting half of the maple syrup in these recipes with pure stevia extract powder. Using the microscoop that comes with the stevia (⅓₂ tsp), I add 2 scoops, or if you prefer you could eliminate the maple syrup altogether and use stevia (4–5 scoops).

Making Nondairy Milks

Making your own plant-based milk couldn't be easier, especially if you have a high-powered blender. Seriously, once you try fresh almond milk, you'll never buy it at the store again, and it's much more affordable. The process for making different plant-based milks is very similar for much of what you can choose from at the store, like almond and coconut milk—the ratio is simply 1:4 nuts to water.

For example, to make almond milk, add 1 cup of raw almonds to a high-speed blender with 4 cups of water and blend for several minutes. Pour the liquid into a bowl through cheesecloth* to strain the almond pump. (*Instead of cheesecloth, I use a nut milk bag, which is washable and reusable; I ordered mine online, and it's lasted over a year so far and only cost 5 dollars.) I like to add 1 Tbsp of liquid sweetener like agave, 1 tsp vanilla extract, and ⅛ tsp salt for a little extra flavor. This recipe is enough to fill a 1-quart Mason jar and lasts about 3–4 days in the refrigerator. So think about that boxed almond milk on the store shelf: Unopened, it will last for months. Once you open it, it's good for a few weeks in the fridge. Whatever they need to do to make something fresh last for weeks isn't something I want to put in my body.

I don't usually make plant-based milk like the recipe I just gave, however. Leaving the pulp in is a key to making smoothies that keep you full all morning, and the pulp has a lot of nutrients and fiber. When I make smoothies, I add the water and almonds (or other nuts) with the water and blend that for several minutes, then add the remaining ingredients. Besides, making plant-milks to keep in the fridge is just an extra step and this way you won't have to worry about the milk going bad. Here is a run-down of different plant-based milks:

Almond, oat, macadamia, coconut, and pistachio nut milks are all made the same way with a 1:4 ratio, using raw nuts.

Rice milk is usually made with a similar ratio of cooked brown rice, it has a lot less nutrients than other nut milks, and generally has a lot of sweetener added. That, plus the fact that you usually have to cook the rice first adds more work and planning, where nut milks are so much easier. Also, fresh rice milk has significantly less nutritional value than most nut milks, making it mostly empty calories.

I've tried many ways to make **soymilk**, and in the end it always has different amounts of a beany taste. Like rice milk, making soy milk is just too much planning and work for me; nut milks are so much easier and quicker!

Hemp milk is another plant-based milk I find in stores, and it's the same 1:4 ratio using hemp seeds. It has a stronger taste than many nut milks, which stands out too much in smoothies for my taste.

Cashew milk is unique in that there is very little pulp after blending the 1:4 ratio for several minutes, and it has a fairly neutral taste. Soaking cashews overnight makes them very soft for blending, which helps a lot if you don't have a high-powered blender.

Peanut milk can be made with a 1:4 ratio like cashews (no pulp is left after blending). It's best to use dry-roasted peanuts instead of raw, since raw peanuts have a stronger, raw flavor that doesn't mix well with other ingredients.

Acknowledgments

My two boys, Carrick and Gareth, are the reason I wrote this cookbook. Now wherever you go in life, you can bring with you the healthy tastes you grew up on. You are two bright lights in the world!

I began cooking as a teenager, and my mom's interest in exploring different foods helped to inspire me, so thank you, Mom! And as always, my sister Marcie has been my biggest cheerleader in whatever I do.

Without the support and inspiration of these women, this cookbook would never have been written: Jennifer Moore, Jackie Rose, Jenn Broman, Sherrill Sasser, Betsy Perry, Victoria Mangus, Mary Rubino, and Sarah Stowell.

Proofreading this book was no small investment of time and energy, so thank you to Beth Gaudette, Tom Culhane, and my sister Marcie for helping me form this book!

Thanks to everyone who has come to the cooking classes I've been teaching for the last several years, helping to inspire me to write new recipes and encouraging me to write this cookbook!

I'd like to thank Vegan Publishers for taking this book on and for being a springboard to help me bring my recipes and my cooking system to a much larger audience.

Thanks to David Moulton for many of the photos in this book, and to Rachel Adams for the beautiful cover designs.

Appendix:
For My Fellow Vegans

There are many forms of vegan advocacy—some people go to protests, some show documentaries to groups, and some people teach cooking classes.

We've done a great job of raising awareness about veganism so far—twenty years ago, any time I ate at a restaurant I had to explain what vegan meant to the wait staff, whereas now it feels like common knowledge. The annual Vegfests near me keep upgrading to bigger venues because of the crowds of interested people—a great problem to have! And the choices of vegan products now compared to twenty years ago is tremendous!

I'd like to make the case for more cooking classes as vegan advocacy. When people ask me what I eat, and I go through the list of fruits, veggies, beans, nuts, legumes, et cetera, I can almost see the wincing. Yeah, it sounds super healthy but not exactly super appetizing; we need to show them that it's not boring!

You don't need to be a trained chef or a nutritionist to teach cooking classes. If you are vegan and you like to cook, you probably already know a lot more about vegan cooking than most people. Another thing to keep in mind is that you can teach any recipes you want, whether they're yours or someone else's.

Here are a few suggestions for getting started teaching vegan cooking classes in your area: If you've never taught cooking classes before, your biggest initial hurdle is probably going to be credibility. You need to get your foot in the door somewhere, to have a starting point to build on. I've had the most luck teaching in places that don't traditionally have cooking classes, places that don't have commercial kitchens to use. Libraries are a good place to start; they are often looking for public events to add to their calendars, and they likely already have at least a handful of books about healthy eating, so you can highlight that tie-in. I would suggest offering to teach several classes for free, but ask to be reimbursed for the cost of the ingredients. You'll need to bring your kitchen to them. The Vitamix, food processor, and Instant Pot all come with me, and I can make whatever I need as long as I have a table and someplace to plug in. The library directors in my area all know each other, so once I was able to teach a few classes at the library in my town, I could use the library director as a reference and the word spread quickly.

Once you've taught some library classes, you can plan ahead with the libraries and put more classes on your calendar; they like to schedule months ahead. Libraries usually have at least a small budget for speakers and events, so you might even make a little money while you're at it!

Once you've taught some classes and established some credibility, consider branching out and seeking out groups of people who are interested in healthy eating, and see if you can work with them. Health and wellness centers, yoga studios, et cetera, already have a client base and are promoting healthy lifestyles, so they already have built-in audiences. Being able to bring your classes and equipment to their space is a big plus for them too since it makes it easy for them. Post your cooking classes on social media, which in turn does some cross-promotion for those places where you're teaching. They'd be happy for your help in spreading the word about their work too!

Several other groups I would recommend contacting and working with are other vegetarian groups, parenting groups, and religious centers. If you aren't already part of a vegetarian group in your area, look online for a local meet-up group that has regular events. That's going to be a group already very much in line with what you'd be teaching, and it's a quick and easy way for them to find out about your classes. Organized parents' groups often have a focus on health and nutrition for kids, and there are plenty of tie-ins for vegan cooking classes to help parents feed their kids healthy and unprocessed foods.

Judging from the local church bulletins of sausage breakfasts and donut coffee hours, they could use some help moving in a healthier direction. Churches and other religious centers are another example of communities of people who already come together regularly for events, so they're a great way to reach people who may not be familiar with the way you cook but are interested in being healthier. Church leaders care about the health and wellness of the members of the congregation, so you may get interest in being able to help show their community a healthier way to live.

Try approaching supermarkets in your area about doing some cooking demos or classes in the store. You would be helping to show *their customers* how to use *their products* to make delicious and healthy recipes. Plus, supermarkets often want to show that they are giving back to the communities they're in. If you have a local community paper, the supermarkets probably already have a good relationship with the paper, and cooking classes can be free advertising for them in the paper and a great way show their local support—a win-win-win for everyone. Better to go with an independent supermarket if possible, since the large chain supermarkets have a lot of regulations and layers of corporate permission you'll need to go through, but it's certainly worth a try!

Another way to teach cooking classes is to do home parties, or cooking classes in people's homes with a group of their friends and family. This is a fun and more informal way to teach classes—you're giving friends an excuse to get together, eat great food, and learn new things! When you teach public classes, make sure to let people know that you also teach for home parties, and they'll be excited to get their friends together to share what they just learned. Signing up for a public cooking class is daunting to a lot of people because they might not know anyone there and won't know what to expect, so home parties give people a chance to be more comfortable. Also, I like to have some classes that I only teach as home parties, which can be a fun change of pace. Make sure to bring a gift for the host, like a great vegan cookbook. Make sure to have a written packing list for each class; there's just too much to have to remember to bring between the food and cooking equipment. It's better to bring everything you will need to use; I even bring a gallon of water because I never know if the tap water where I'm teaching is any good.

The last thing I want to add is that although I teach cooking classes as vegan advocacy, I advertise them as healthy cooking classes and not specifically vegan. I explain in the beginning of the classes that I'm vegan and that I eat a whole-food, plant-based diet, and I do talk a bit about what all that means before I start cooking. And I always put on my vegan apron! People usually ask questions about how I became vegan, plus the usual questions about where I get my protein, getting food cravings, et cetera, and I answer these if I'm asked, but I don't push. As a vegan, maybe you want to shout about it from the rooftops, to stop animal cruelty, to tell people all the healthy and environmental impacts of meat and dairy. I hear you, believe me. But cooking classes are a different kind of advocacy. You're being hosted by groups and individuals that want to learn from you but didn't ask for you to come lecture everyone, and if you're being critical of non-vegans or push hard with the vegan agenda, you probably won't be invited back. So just know your audience; it's a cooking class, not a protest.

Resources

Here are a few great online resources for exploring whole-food, plant based eating further:

OneGreenPlanet.org is a vegan food and activism blog aggregator that culls recipes and articles together into a daily e-mail. I've found lots of inspiration from many of the recipes there! I usually print out the recipes I want to try and stack them up on my kitchen counter, so that when I want to try something new I just work through the pile.

HappyCow.net is my go-to for traveling; this website and mobile app is a great resource for where to find vegan, vegetarian, and veg-friendly restaurants and health food stores.

NutritionFacts.org offers a wealth of information for nutrition and health by Dr. Michael Greger and his small army of non-profit volunteers. In addition to daily short videos and articles that arrive in my inbox, the website is a great resource for the latest in evidence-based nutrition, in addition to his book, *How Not To Die.*

Our bodies want to be healthy and strong, so that should be our default. The human body is an amazing, complex, self-regulating system that, most of the time, can take care of itself, if you give it the best and healthiest foods to work with. Just look at what's in people's carts at the grocery store—the human body is truly amazing in that it can do so much with so little. Just imagine what your body could do with three meals a day of whole-food, plant-based superfuel. Well, don't just imagine; give it a try. Just like I took the challenge twenty years ago, I offer the same to you: one month. There's more than enough here in this book to get you started. Here's to great health and wellness, one of our greatest assets!